Solaris™ 10 ZFS Essentials

Solaris™ 10 ZFS Essentials

Scott Watanabe

Sun Microsystems Press

PRENTICE
HALL

Upper Saddle River, NJ • Boston • Indianapolis • San Francisco
New York • Toronto • Montreal • London • Munich • Paris • Madrid
Capetown • Sydney • Tokyo • Singapore • Mexico City

Many of the designations used by manufacturers and sellers to distinguish their products are claimed as trademarks. Where those designations appear in this book, and the publisher was aware of a trademark claim, the designations have been printed with initial capital letters or in all capitals.

The author and publisher have taken care in the preparation of this book, but make no expressed or implied warranty of any kind and assume no responsibility for errors or omissions. No liability is assumed for incidental or consequential damages in connection with or arising out of the use of the information or programs contained herein.

Sun Microsystems, Inc., has intellectual property rights relating to implementations of the technology described in this publication. In particular, and without limitation, these intellectual property rights may include one or more U.S. patents, foreign patents, or pending applications. Sun, Sun Microsystems, the Sun logo, J2ME, J2EE, Solaris, Java, Javadoc, Java Card, NetBeans, and all Sun and Java based trademarks and logos are trademarks or registered trademarks of Sun Microsystems, Inc., in the United States and other countries. UNIX is a registered trademark in the United States and other countries, exclusively licensed through X/Open Company, Ltd.

THIS PUBLICATION IS PROVIDED "AS IS" WITHOUT WARRANTY OF ANY KIND, EITHER EXPRESS OR IMPLIED, INCLUDING, BUT NOT LIMITED TO, THE IMPLIED WARRANTIES OF MERCHANTABILITY, FITNESS FOR A PARTICULAR PURPOSE, OR NON-INFRINGEMENT. THIS PUBLICATION COULD INCLUDE TECHNICAL INACCURACIES OR TYPOGRAPHICAL ERRORS. CHANGES ARE PERIODICALLY ADDED TO THE INFORMATION HEREIN; THESE CHANGES WILL BE INCORPORATED IN NEW EDITIONS OF THE PUBLICATION. SUN MICROSYSTEMS, INC., MAY MAKE IMPROVEMENTS AND/OR CHANGES IN THE PRODUCT(S) AND/OR THE PROGRAM(S) DESCRIBED IN THIS PUBLICATION AT ANY TIME.

The publisher offers excellent discounts on this book when ordered in quantity for bulk purchases or special sales, which may include electronic versions and/or custom covers and content particular to your business, training goals, marketing focus, and branding interests. For more information, please contact:

U.S. Corporate and Government Sales
(800) 382-3419
corpsales@pearsontechgroup.com

For sales outside the United States please contact:

International Sales
international@pearsoned.com

Visit us on the Web: informit.com/ph

Library of Congress Cataloging-in-Publication Data

Watanabe, Scott.
  Solaris 10 ZFS essentials / Scott Watanabe.
    p.   cm.
  Includes index.
  ISBN 978-0-13-700010-4 (pbk. : alk. paper)
  1. Solaris (Computer file) 2. File organization (Computer science) 3. Database management.
  I. Title.
  QA76.9.F5W38 2009
  005.74—dc22

                                                                              2009044423

ISBN-13: 978-0-13-700010-4
ISBN-10:   0-13-700010-3
Text printed in the United States on recycled paper at Courier in Stoughton, Massachusetts.
First printing, December 2009

Contents

Preface

Solaris™ 10 ZFS Essentials is part of a new series of books on Solaris system administration. It presents the revolutionary ZFS file system that was introduced in the Solaris 10 release. ZFS is a file system that is elegant in its simplicity and in the ease with which it allows system administrators to manage data and storage. Other books in the series are *Solaris™ 10 System Administration Essentials* and *Solaris™ 10 Security Essentials*. The former covers all the breakthrough features of the Solaris 10 operating system in one place, and the latter covers all the features of the Solaris 10 operating system that make it the best choice for meeting the present-day challenges to robust and secure computing.

ZFS offers a dramatic advance in data management with an innovative approach to data integrity, near-zero administration, and a welcome integration of file system and volume management capabilities. The centerpiece of this new architecture is the concept of a virtual storage pool, which decouples the file system from physical storage in the same way that virtual memory abstracts the address space from physical memory, allowing for much more efficient use of storage devices.

In ZFS, storage space is shared dynamically between multiple file systems from a single storage pool and is parceled out of the pool as file systems request it. Physical storage can be added to storage pools dynamically without interrupting services, which provides new levels of flexibility, availability, and performance. And in terms of scalability, ZFS is a 128-bit file system. Its theoretical limits are truly mind-boggling—2,128 bytes of storage and 264 for everything else, including file systems, snapshots, directory entries, devices, and more. And ZFS implements an improvement on RAID-5 by introducing RAID-Z, which uses parity, striping, and atomic operations to ensure reconstruction of corrupted data. It is ideally suited for managing industry-standard storage servers.

Books in the Solaris System Administration Series

The following sections talk more about the other two books in the series.

Solaris™ 10 System Administration Essentials

Solaris™ 10 System Administration Essentials covers all the breakthrough features of the Solaris 10 operating system in one place. It does so in a straightforward way that makes an enterprise-level operating system accessible to system administrators at all levels.

The book provides a comprehensive overview along with hands-on examples of the key features that have made Solaris the leading UNIX operating system for years, and it covers the significant new features of Solaris 10 that put it far ahead of its competitors, such as Zones, the ZFS file system, Fault Management Architecture, Service Management Facility, and DTrace (the dynamic tracing tool for troubleshooting OS and application problems on production systems in real time).

Solaris™ 10 Security Essentials

Solaris™ 10 Security Essentials covers all the security features and technologies in the Solaris 10 operating system that make it the OS of choice for IT environments that require optimum security.

The book explains the strengths of Solaris operating system security—its scalability and adaptability—in a simple, straightforward way. It explains how security features in Solaris can protect a single-user system with login authentication as well as how those features can protect Internet and intranet configurations.

Intended Audience

The three books in the Solaris System Administration Series can benefit anyone who wants to learn more about the Solaris 10 operating system. They are written to be particularly accessible to system administrators who are new to Solaris, as well as to people who are perhaps already serving as administrators in companies running Linux, Windows, and other UNIX systems.

If you are not currently a practicing system administrator but want to become one, this series, starting with *Solaris™ 10 System Administration Essentials*, provides an excellent introduction. In fact, most of the examples used in the books are suited to or can be adapted to small learning environments such as a home setup. So, even before you venture into corporate system administration or deploy Solaris 10 in your existing IT installation, these books will help you experiment in a small test environment.

OpenSolaris

In June 2005, Sun Microsystems introduced OpenSolaris, a fully functional Solaris operating system release built from open source. Although the books in this series focus on Solaris 10, they often incorporate aspects of OpenSolaris. Now that Solaris has been open-sourced, its evolution has accelerated even beyond its normally rapid pace. The authors of this series have often found it interesting to introduce features or nuances that are new in OpenSolaris. At the same, many of the enhancements introduced into OpenSolaris are finding their way into Solaris 10. So, whether you are learning Solaris 10 or already have an eye on OpenSolaris, the books in this series are for you.

Acknowledgments

Any good book always results from more than just the effort of the attributed author, and this book is far from being an exception. I have benefited from the tremendous support of Cindy Swearingen and Jeff Ramsey. Cindy provided insight and guidance without which this book simply would not have been possible. She critiqued my ideas and writing diplomatically, and she offered great ideas of her own.

Jeff took my rough drawings and created detailed illustrations, upon which the figures in this book are based. If they are not clear in any way, that is no fault of Jeff's. As always, he was a pleasure to work with.

I would like to thank Todd Lowry, Uzzal Dewan, and the rest of the staff at Sun's RLDC for allowing me access to equipment for testing and showing me how they use ZFS in their operation. Thanks to Dean Kemp for being my technical sounding board and giving the opportunity to use my knowledge of ZFS to resolve some real-world problems.

A big thank you to Jim Siwila for jumping in with editorial support at critical points during challenging times at Sun. Thanks to Judy Hall at Sun for her support and presenting me with the opportunity to write this book.

To my family and friends, thank you for your understanding and support.

About the Author

Scott Watanabe is a freelance consultant with more than twenty-five years in the computer/IT industry. Scott has worked for Sun Microsystems for more than eleven years and has worked with Sun technology since the mid-1980s. Scott has also worked as a systems administrator for more than ten years and as a systems manager for a few of those years. While at Sun, Scott worked as a chief architect for Utility Computing, a backline engineer in Network Technical Support, and a lead course developer for Internal Technical Training.

Introducing ZFS File Systems

This chapter introduces ZFS, a new kind of file system from Sun Microsystems that is elegant in its simplicity, particularly in the way that you can easily manage data and storage. The ZFS file system is available in the following Solaris releases:

- *Solaris 10 6/06 release (ZFS root and install features available in Solaris 10 10/08 release)*
- *OpenSolaris 2008.11 release (includes ZFS root and install features)*

1.1 Overview of ZFS

ZFS is an all-purpose file system that is built on top of a pool of storage devices. ZFS doesn't use a middle layer of virtualized volumes like other volume management products. This means you can easily aggregate your storage components with a few ZFS commands.

File systems that are created from a storage pool share space with the other file systems in the pool. You don't have to allocate storage space based on the intended size of a file system because file systems grow automatically within the space that is allocated to the storage pool. When new storage devices are added, all file systems in the pool can immediately use the additional space.

ZFS provides the following redundancy configurations:

- Mirror
- RAID-Z (single parity), also called RAID-Z1
- RAID-Z2 (double parity)

RAID-Z is similar to RAID-5 but uses a variable-stripe width to eliminate the RAID-5 write hole (stripe corruption due to a loss of power between data and parity updates). All RAID-Z writes are full-stripe writes. See Jeff Bonwick's blog on RAID-Z at http://blogs.sun.com/bonwick/entry/raid_z.

Additionally, 256 checksums on data blocks protect data against corruption. Using disk scrubbing on live-disk ZFS can detect errors that otherwise go undetected and that can be corrected before the data is lost. See Eric Lowe's entry on silent data corruption at http://blogs.sun.com/elowe/entry/zfs_saves_the_day_ta.

ZFS is a smarter file system. If it detects damaged data, it will go back and retrieve another copy of the data. You can enable another layer of redundancy in the ZFS file system by increasing the number of copies of data written to disk in the file system. This feature was added to Solaris 10 10/08.

ZFS also provides built-in compression. Compression reduces the amount of I/O to the disk by two to three times by reducing the amount of data written. You can select different compression algorithms depending on the workload and data stored.

Additionally, ZFS supports raw volumes. Now applications that require raw devices can take advantage of ZFS. You can use ZFS for swap devices, and it is installed by default when selecting ZFS as the root file system.

1.1.1 Advantages of Using ZFS

The advantages of using ZFS are numerous:

- Data inconsistency detection and recovery are provided by ZFS redundancy features. ZFS guarantees data integrity from disk to memory and from memory to disk. See Bonwick's blog at http://blogs.sun.com/bonwick/en_US/entry/zfs_end_to_end_data.
- It is easy to set up a mirrored ZFS root pool configuration so that you don't need additional volume management products to provide this feature.
- ZFS boot environments are created instantly and can be used for patching and upgrading.
- ZFS makes it easy to create and manage file systems without needing complex command strings or editing multiple configuration files.

- ZFS makes it easy to set up file system quotas or reservations, turn compression on or off, or set other characteristics per file system.

- ZFS provides constant-time snapshots so that an administrator or users can roll back copies of the data.

- ZFS makes it possible to delegate administration directly to users. Using the RBAC facility, ZFS administration can be delegated to users.

- ZFS provides automation of mundane tasks. Once a ZFS file system is created, Solaris will remember to mount the file system on reboot.

- ZFS provides a history of commands used on a pool or file system.

1.1.2 A Top-Level View of ZFS

To get a better understanding of ZFS, it helps to see the whole before talking about the parts of ZFS. ZFS can be split into two major parts: the ZFS pool and the ZFS datasets. The zpool command manages the ZFS pool, and the zfs command manages the ZFS datasets. Each of these commands has subcommands that manage each part from cradle to grave.

The fundamental base of ZFS is the ZFS pool. A **pool** is the primary storage element that supports the ZFS datasets, as illustrated in Figure 1.1. The pool acts much like the memory of a computer system. When a dataset needs another chunk, ZFS will allocate more storage from the pool. When a file is deleted, the free storage returns to the pool for all datasets in the pool to use.

Figure 1.1 The base of ZFS: the pool

A ZFS pool can contain many ZFS datasets, as shown in Figure 1.2. Each dataset can grow and shrink as needed. Using snapshots, quotas, and reservations can affect how much each dataset can consume of the ZFS pool.

ZFS supports three datasets:

- **ZFS file system**: A file system that is mounted for normal usage (such as home directories or data storage)

- **Volume**: Raw volumes that can be used for swap and dump partitions in a ZFS boot configuration

- **Clone**: A copy of a ZFS file system or volume

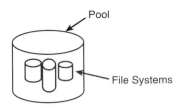

Figure 1.2 The ZFS pool with three ZFS datasets

At a minimum, a single virtual device (*vdev*) is needed for a ZFS pool (see Figure 1.3). A vdev can comprise a file, a slice of a disk, the whole disk, or even a logical disk from a hardware array or another volume product such as Solaris Volume Manager. A vdev supports three redundancy configurations: mirror, RAID-Z, and RAID-Z2.

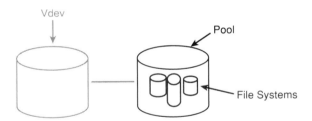

Figure 1.3 ZFS pool with a single vdev

In Figure 1.4, the vdev contains a mirrored array made up of two whole disks. ZFS can handle disks of similar size and different disk geometries. This feature is good for a home system, where if a disk fails, the replacement disk doesn't have to be of the same make and model. The only requirement of a replacement disk is that it must be the same capacity or larger.

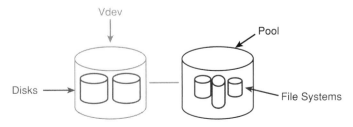

Figure 1.4 A vdev with a mirrored array supporting a ZFS pool

Increasing the storage of a ZFS pool is simple. You just add another vdev. In Figure 1.5, a second mirrored vdev is concatenated to the pool. You can increase a ZFS pool at any time, and you don't need to adjust any of the datasets contained within the pool.

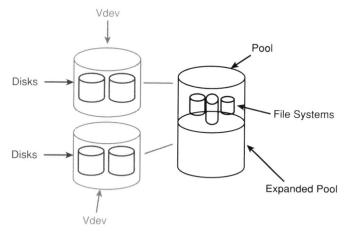

Figure 1.5 Concatenation of a second mirrored vdev to the ZFS pool

Once a ZFS pool is expanded, the data sets in the pool can take advantage of the increased size. ZFS will take advantage of the expanded storage and distribute the new writes across all the disk spindles (see Figure 1.6).

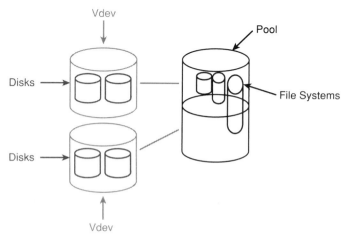

Figure 1.6 File system expanding in the larger ZFS pool

1.2 Fast and Simple Storage

ZFS was designed to be fast and simple with only two commands to remember: `zpool` and `zfs`. You can create a ZFS pool and have a writable file system in one step. To create the configuration in Figure 1.4, you just execute the following command:

```
$ time pfexec zpool create mpool mirror c5t0d0 c5t1d0
real   0m6.155s
user   0m0.216s
sys    0m1.456s
```

By using the `time` command, you can see it took six seconds to create a new ZFS pool. In this example you used the `pfexec` command to execute the `zpool` command as root. You can then view the status of the new ZFS pool by running the following command:

```
$ zpool status mpool
  pool: mpool
 state: ONLINE
 scrub: none requested
config:

    NAME        STATE      READ WRITE CKSUM
    mpool       ONLINE        0     0     0
      mirror    ONLINE        0     0     0
        c5t0d0  ONLINE        0     0     0
        c5t1d0  ONLINE        0     0     0

errors: No known data errors
```

With the previous code, you have created a new pool called *mpool* with a new virtual device that consists of two disks in mirror configuration. At this point, you can write to the newly mounted file system:

```
$ df -h | grep mpool
mpool                     85M    18K    85M    1% /mpool
$ pfexec touch /mpool/j
$ ls -l /mpool/j
-rw-r--r-- 1 root root 0 2009-04-24 01:20 /mpool/j
```

Just by using one command line, you created a mirrored pool and mounted it.

1.3 ZFS Commands

ZFS has only two commands. The zpool command creates, modifies, and destroys ZFS pools. The zfs command creates, modifies, and destroys ZFS file systems. In this book, Chapters 2 and 5 are dedicated to administration of ZFS pools, and the other chapters use the zfs command as part of the administrative tasks.

2

Managing Storage Pools

ZFS storage pools are the basis of the ZFS system. In this chapter, I cover the basic concepts, configurations, and administrative tasks of ZFS pools. In Chapter 5, I cover advanced configuration topics in ZFS pool administration.

The zpool *command manages ZFS storage pools. The* zpool *command creates, modifies, and destroys ZFS pools.*

*Redundant configurations supported in ZFS are mirror (RAID-1), RAID-Z (similar to RAID-5), and RAID-Z2 with a double parity (similar to RAID-6). All traditional RAID-5-like algorithms (RAID-4, RAID-6, RDP, and EVEN-ODD, for example) suffer from a problem known as the **RAID-5 write hole**. If only part of a RAID-5 stripe is written and power is lost before all blocks have made it to disk, the parity will remain out of sync with the data (and is therefore useless) forever, unless a subsequent full-stripe write overwrites it. In RAID-Z, ZFS uses variable-width RAID stripes so that all writes are full-stripe writes. This design is possible only because ZFS integrates file system and device management in such a way that the file system's metadata has enough information about the underlying data redundancy model to handle variable-width RAID stripes. RAID-Z is the world's first software-only solution to the RAID-5 write hole.*

2.1 ZFS Pool Concepts

ZFS pools are comprised of virtual devices. ZFS abstracts every physical device into a virtual device. A vdev can be a disk, a slice of a disk, a file, or even a logical volume presented by another volume manager such as Solaris Volume Manager (SVM) or a LUN from a hardware RAID device.

These are the virtual devices types:

- **Dynamic stripe**: A dynamic stripe is a nonredundant configuration of a simple disk or concatenation of disks.
- **Redundant group (mirror, RAID-Z1, or RAID-Z2)**: A mirror can be a two-way or three-way mirror. RAID-Z groups are recommended to have up to nine disks in the group. If there are more, then multiple vdevs are recommended. Two disks minimum are needed for RAID-Z, and three disks at a minimum are needed for RAID-Z2. (Note that *RAID-Z* and *RAID-Z1* are interchangeable terms. With the introduction of the RAID-Z2 feature, the term *RAID-Z* evolved into *RAID-Z1* to differentiate it from RAID-Z2. I use both terms in this book.)
- **Spare**: A spare vdev is for a hot standby disk replacement.
- **Log**: A log vdev is for ZFS Intent Log (ZIL). The ZIL increases the write performance on ZFS. Only dynamic stripe and mirrored vdev configurations are supported for this vdev type.
- **Cache**: A cache vdev is used to speed up random reads from a RAID-Z-configured pool. Its intended use is for read-heavy workloads. There is no redundancy support at this point for this vdev type. If there is a read error, then ZFS will read from the original storage pool.

Log and cache vdevs are used with solid-state disks (SSDs) in the Sun Storage 7000 series in hybrid storage pools (HSPs; see `http://blogs.sun.com/ahl/entry/fishworks_launch`).

Best-practice guidelines for ZFS pools include the following:

- Mirrored configuration beyond a three-way mirror should not be used. Think about using a RAID-Z configuration instead.
- Use RAID-Z or RAID-Z2 virtual device groups with fewer than ten disks in each vdev.
- Using whole disks is best. ZFS works best with "just a bunch of disks" (JBOD).
- Use slices for vdev groups only for boot disks.
- Use disks of a terabyte or less for boot devices.
- Use matched-capacity disks (mixed geometry is OK) for the best maximum storage results.
- Use matching sizes of vdevs in a ZFS pool. Match the number of disks and redundancy groups in each vdev in a pool for best performance.

Creating/adding new vdevs to a ZFS pool is the most unforgiving part about ZFS. Once committed, some operations cannot be undone. The `zpool` command will warn you, however, if the operation is not what's expected. There is a `force` option in `zpool` to bypass any of the warnings, but it is not recommended that you use the `force` option unless you are sure you will not need to reverse the operation.

These are the rules for ZFS pools:

- Once a normal (dynamic stripe) vdev is added to a ZFS pool, it cannot be removed.

- Only the special-use vdevs can be removed: spares, log, and cache.

- Disks the same size or larger can be replaced within a vdev.

- Disks can be added to a single disk or mirrored vdev to form a mirror or a three-way mirror.

- New disks cannot be added to an existing RAID-Z or RAID-Z2 vdev configuration.

2.2 Creating a Dynamic Stripe

A dynamic stripe is the most basic pool that can be created. There is no redundancy in this configuration. If any disk fails, then the whole pool is lost. Any pool created with multiple vdevs will dynamically stripe across each vdev or physical device.

You can use the `zpool` command with the subcommand to create a dynamic stripe. After the `create` subcommand is the name of the new ZFS pool, dstripe, and the disks that will comprise the pool.

```
# zpool create dstripe c5t0d0 c5t1d0
```

The following listing presents the results of creating the ZFS pool dstripe. On line 2, `zpool list` is executed to list all the ZFS pools on the system. Line 3 starts a list of the available pools. The command gives you general information about the ZFS pools.

```
1  # zpool create dstripe c5t0d0 c5t1d0
2  # zpool list
3  NAME      SIZE    USED   AVAIL    CAP   HEALTH  ALTROOT
4  dstripe   234M     75K    234M     0%   ONLINE  -
5  rpool    15.9G   3.21G   12.7G    20%   ONLINE  -
```

Next on line 6, `zpool status` is issued to inquire about the status of the ZFS pools. Starting at line 7, the status of the ZFS pool dstripe is displayed, with a normal status. Reading the `config:` section of the output starting at line 10, the pool dstripe is shown as two concatenated disks. Lines 14 and 15 list the vdevs (c5t0d0 and c5t1d0) that belong to the pool dstripe. The second pool listed is made of a single disk called *rpool,* configured as a dynamic stripe with only a single vdev (c3d0s0). It was created as part of the OS installation process.

```
 6   # zpool status
 7   pool: dstripe
 8   state: ONLINE
 9   scrub: none requested
10   config:
11
12           NAME        STATE     READ WRITE CKSUM
13           dstripe     ONLINE       0     0     0
14             c5t0d0    ONLINE       0     0     0
15             c5t1d0    ONLINE       0     0     0
16
17   errors: No known data errors
18
19     pool: rpool
20    state: ONLINE
21    scrub: none requested
22   config:
23
24           NAME        STATE     READ WRITE CKSUM
25           rpool       ONLINE       0     0     0
26             c3d0s0    ONLINE       0     0     0
27
28   errors: No known data errors
```

Figure 2.1 illustrates the resulting dynamic pool with its two vdevs of single nonredundant disks. Any problems with the disks (sector errors or disk failure) may result in the loss of the whole pool or data.

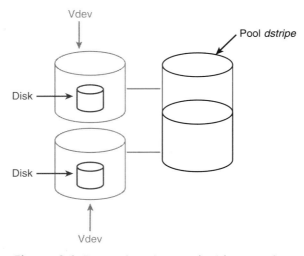

Figure 2.1 Dynamic stripe pool with two vdevs

2.3 Creating a Pool with Mirrored Devices

The following command creates a ZFS mirrored pool called *mpool* with a mirrored vdev. As expected, the new pool mpool is about half the capacity of dstripe. The pool dstripe is a concatenation of two disks of the same capacity, and mpool is a mirror of a disk of the same capacity.

The following command line shows how to use the `zpool` command with the subcommand `create` to create a pool with mirrored vdevs. After the `create` subcommand is the name of the new ZFS pool, mpool. The `mirror` subcommand will create a mirrored vdev with the disks c5t2d0 and c5t3d0.

`zpool create mpool mirror c5t2d0 c5t3d0`

The following output is the creation of a mirrored ZFS pool called *mpool*. Using the `zpool list` command, you now can see the capacity of the newly created pool on line 5. Notice it is half the capacity of the dstripe pool.

```
1   # zpool create mpool mirror c5t2d0 c5t3d0
2   # zpool list
3   NAME      SIZE    USED   AVAIL    CAP   HEALTH   ALTROOT
4   dstripe   234M     75K    234M     0%   ONLINE   -
5   mpool     117M   73.5K    117M     0%   ONLINE   -
6   rpool    15.9G   3.21G    12.7G   20%   ONLINE   -
```

Starting at line 20 (in the following part of the listing) is the status information of mpool. The disks c5t2d0 and c5t3d0 are configured as a mirror vdev, and the mirror is part of *mpool*. This is an important concept in reading the status information of ZFS pools. Notice the indentations on the pool name notations. The first is the name of the ZFS pool. Then at the first indentation of the name are the vdevs that are part of the pool. In the case of a dynamic stripe, this is the physical device. If the pool is created with redundant vdev(s), the first indentation will be `mirror`, `raidz1`, or `raidz2`. Then the next indentation will be the physical devices that comprise the redundant vdev. On lines 13 and 25 are the names dstripe and mpool, respectively. On lines 14 and 15 are the disks that belong to dstripe on the first indentation. On line 25 is the mirror configuration, and the next indented line lists the disks belonging to the mirror configuration. Compare Figures 2.1 and 2.2 for a graphical representation of each pool's configuration.

```
7    # zpool status
8    pool: dstripe
9    state: ONLINE
10   scrub: none requested
11   config:
```

continues

```
12
13          NAME          STATE     READ WRITE CKSUM
14          dstripe       ONLINE       0    0    0
15            c5t0d0      ONLINE       0    0    0
16            c5t1d0      ONLINE       0    0    0
17
18  errors: No known data errors
19
20    pool: mpool
21   state: ONLINE
22   scrub: none requested
23  config:
24          NAME          STATE     READ WRITE CKSUM
25          mpool         ONLINE       0    0    0
26            mirror      ONLINE       0    0    0
27              c5t2d0    ONLINE       0    0    0
28              c5t3d0    ONLINE       0    0    0
29
30  errors: No known data errors
31
32    pool: rpool
33   state: ONLINE
34   scrub: none requested
35  config:
36
37          NAME          STATE     READ WRITE CKSUM
38          rpool         ONLINE       0    0    0
39            c3d0s0      ONLINE       0    0    0
40  errors: No known data errors
```

Figure 2.2 illustrates the results of creating the ZFS pool mpool with one mirrored vdev.

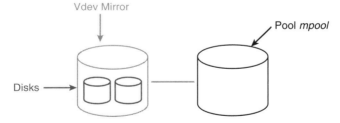

Figure 2.2 Pool *mpool* with a mirrored vdev

The following sequence adds a second mirror vdev to the pool, doubling the size of pool mpool. Notice that after the addition of the second mirror vdev, the dstripe and mpool pools are the same capacity. Line 30 is the mirrored vdev with the physical disks c5t4d0 and c5t5d0 indented.

```
1.  # zpool add mpool mirror c5t4d0 c5t5d0
2.  # zpool list
3.  NAME      SIZE    USED    AVAIL    CAP   HEALTH   ALTROOT
4.  dstripe   234M    75K     234M     0%    ONLINE   -
```

continues

```
 5.  mpool      234M     78K    234M      0%  ONLINE  -
 6.  rpool     15.9G   3.21G   12.7G     20%  ONLINE  -
 7.  # zpool status
 8.       pool: dstripe
 9.      state: ONLINE
10.   scrub: none requested
11. config:
12.
13. NAME         STATE      READ WRITE CKSUM
14. dstripe      ONLINE        0     0     0
15.   c5t0d0     ONLINE        0     0     0
16.   c5t1d0     ONLINE        0     0     0
17.
18. errors: No known data errors
19.
20.    pool: mpool
21.   state: ONLINE
22.   scrub: none requested
23. config:
24.
25. NAME         STATE      READ WRITE CKSUM
26. mpool        ONLINE        0     0     0
27.   mirror     ONLINE        0     0     0
28.     c5t2d0   ONLINE        0     0     0
29.     c5t3d0   ONLINE        0     0     0
30.   mirror     ONLINE        0     0     0
31.     c5t4d0   ONLINE        0     0     0
32.     c5t5d0   ONLINE        0     0     0
33.
34. errors: No known data errors
35.
36.    pool: rpool
37.   state: ONLINE
38.   scrub: none requested
39. config:
40. NAME         STATE      READ WRITE CKSUM
41. rpool        ONLINE        0     0     0
42.   c3d0s0     ONLINE        0     0     0

43. errors: No known data errors
```

Figure 2.3 shows the results of adding a second mirrored vdev to ZFS pool *mpool*.

2.4 Creating a Pool with RAID-Z Devices

In ZFS you can also create redundant vdevs similar to RAID-5, called *RAID-Z*. To create a pool with double parity, you would use RAID-Z2 instead.

The following command line will create a ZFS pool named *rzpool* with two RAID-Z1 vdevs, each with four disks:

```
# zpool create rzpool raidz1 c5t6d0 c5t7d0 c5t8d0 c5t9d0 raidz1
c5t10d0 c5t11d0 c5t12d0 c5t13d0
```

The first RAID-Z1 vdev consists of disks c5t6d0, c5t7d0, c5t8d0, and c5t9d0, and the second RAID-Z1 vdev has c5t6d0, c5t7d0, c5t8d0, and c5t9d0 as members.

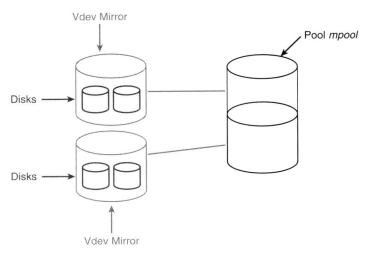

Figure 2.3 Pool *mpool* with the added mirror vdev

The `zpool list` command shows the summary status of the new pool rzpool. The output of `zpool status`, on lines 16 and 21, shows the RAID-Z1 virtual devices and physical disk devices that make up each RAID-Z1 virtual device.

```
 1   # zpool create rzpool raidz1 c5t6d0 c5t7d0 c5t8d0 c5t9d0
raidz1 c5t10d0 c5t11d0 c5t12d0 c5t13d0
 2   # zpool list
 3   NAME       SIZE    USED   AVAIL    CAP   HEALTH  ALTROOT
 4   dstripe    234M    75K    234M     0%    ONLINE  -
 5   mpool      234M    78K    234M     0%    ONLINE  -
 6   rpool      15.9G   3.21G  12.7G    20%   ONLINE  -
 7   rzpool     936M    138K   936M     0%    ONLINE  -
 8   # zpool status
     …lines deleted…
 9   pool: rzpool
10    state: ONLINE
11    scrub: none requested
12   config:
13
14           NAME          STATE    READ WRITE CKSUM
15           rzpool        ONLINE      0     0     0
16             raidz1      ONLINE      0     0     0
17               c5t6d0    ONLINE      0     0     0
18               c5t7d0    ONLINE      0     0     0
19               c5t8d0    ONLINE      0     0     0
20               c5t9d0    ONLINE      0     0     0
21             raidz1      ONLINE      0     0     0
22               c5t10d0   ONLINE      0     0     0
23               c5t11d0   ONLINE      0     0     0
24               c5t12d0   ONLINE      0     0     0
25               c5t13d0   ONLINE      0     0     0
26
27   errors: No known data errors
```

Figure 2.4 has two RAID-Z1 vdevs with four physical disks to each vdev. The vdevs are concatenated to form the ZFS pool rzpool.

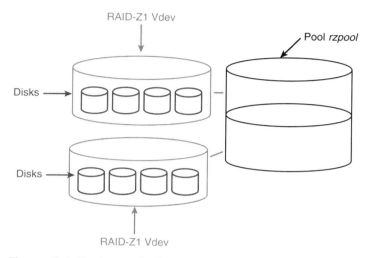

Figure 2.4 Pool *rzpool* using two RAID-Z1 redundant vdevs

2.5 Creating a Spare in a Storage Pool

You can add spare vdevs to a pool to increase its reliability and maintain performance. In case of disk failure, ZFS can replace failed disks with spare disks automatically. This gives the administrator time to make repairs without compromising the reliability and performance of the pool. Spares can be shared among multiple pools. The following example adds a spare disk device to the pool *mpool*. On line 22, the spare vdev is now listed as part of the pool *mpool*.

```
1   # zpool add mpool spare c5t14d0
2   # zpool list
3   NAME       SIZE    USED   AVAIL    CAP  HEALTH  ALTROOT
4   dstripe    234M     75K    234M     0%  ONLINE  -
5   mpool      234M     84K    234M     0%  ONLINE  -
6   rpool     15.9G   3.20G   12.7G    20%  ONLINE  -
7   rzpool     936M    141K    936M     0%  ONLINE  -
8   # zpool status mpool
9     pool: mpool
10    state: ONLINE
11    scrub: none requested
```

continues

```
12  config:
13
14        NAME          STATE     READ WRITE CKSUM
15        mpool         ONLINE       0    0    0
16          mirror      ONLINE       0    0    0
17            c5t2d0    ONLINE       0    0    0
18            c5t3d0    ONLINE       0    0    0
19          mirror      ONLINE       0    0    0
20            c5t4d0    ONLINE       0    0    0
21            c5t5d0    ONLINE       0    0    0
22        spares
23          c5t14d0     AVAIL
24
25  errors: No known data errors
```

In Figure 2.5, an additional vdev is added to the ZFS pool mpool. A spare vdev can be shared with multiple ZFS pools. The spares must have at least the same capacity of the smallest disk in the other vdev devices.

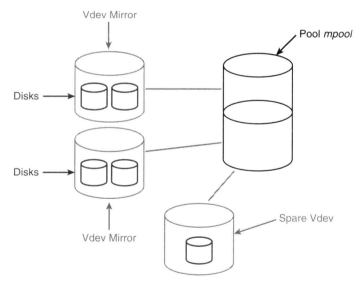

Figure 2.5 Pool *mpool* with a spare vdev added

2.6 Adding a Spare Vdev to a Second Storage Pool

As indicated earlier in the chapter, you can share a spare vdev with other pools on the same system. In the following example, the spare vdev (c5t14d0) disk is shared with ZFS pool *rzpool*. After you add the spare to the *rzpool,* the spare disk now appears in ZFS pools *mpool* and *rzpool,* namely, on lines 16 and 17 and lines 38 and 39.

```
1    # zpool add rzpool spare c5t14d0
2    # zpool status mpool rzpool
3    pool: mpool
4    state: ONLINE
5    scrub: none requested
6    config:
7
8    NAME         STATE      READ WRITE CKSUM
9    mpool        ONLINE        0     0     0
10   mirror       ONLINE        0     0     0
11     c5t2d0     ONLINE        0     0     0
12     c5t3d0     ONLINE        0     0     0
13   mirror       ONLINE        0     0     0
14     c5t4d0     ONLINE        0     0     0
15     c5t5d0     ONLINE        0     0     0
16   spares
17     c5t14d0    AVAIL
18
19   errors: No known data errors
20
21   pool: rzpool
22   state: ONLINE
23   scrub: none requested
24   config:
25
26   NAME          STATE      READ WRITE CKSUM
27   rzpool        ONLINE        0     0     0
28     raidz1      ONLINE        0     0     0
29       c5t6d0    ONLINE        0     0     0
30       c5t7d0    ONLINE        0     0     0
31       c5t8d0    ONLINE        0     0     0
32       c5t9d0    ONLINE        0     0     0
33     raidz1      ONLINE        0     0     0
34       c5t10d0   ONLINE        0     0     0
35       c5t11d0   ONLINE        0     0     0
36       c5t12d0   ONLINE        0     0     0
37       c5t13d0   ONLINE        0     0     0
38     spares
39       c5t14d0   AVAIL
40
41   errors: No known data errors
```

In Figure 2.6, the spare vdev is shared between the *mpool* and *rzpool* ZFS pools. Each pool can use the spare when needed.

2.7 Replacing Bad Devices Automatically

ZFS has the capability to replace a disk in a pool automatically without intervention by the administrator. This feature, known as **autoreplace**, is turned off by default. This feature will allow ZFS to replace a bad disk with a spare from the spares pool, automatically allowing the pool to operate at optimum performance.

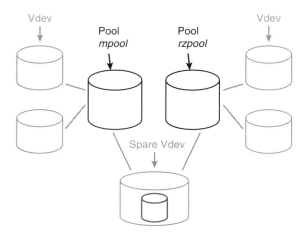

Figure 2.6 Pools *mpool* and *rzpool* sharing a spare vdev

This allows the administrator to replace the failed drive at a later time. The manual disk replacement procedure is covered later in this chapter.

If you list the properties of the ZFS pool, you can see that the autoreplace feature is turned off using the `get` subcommand.

```
1    # zpool get all mpool
2    NAME    PROPERTY        VALUE        SOURCE
3    mpool   size            234M         -
4    mpool   used            111K         -
5    mpool   available       234M         -
6    mpool   capacity        0%           -
7    mpool   altroot         -            default
8    mpool   health          DEGRADED     -
9    mpool   guid            11612108450022771594  -
10   mpool   version         13           default
11   mpool   bootfs          -            default
12   mpool   delegation      on           default
13   mpool   autoreplace     off          default
14   mpool   cachefile       -            default
15   mpool   failmode        wait         default
16   mpool   listsnapshots   off          default
```

To turn on the autoreplace feature, use the following command line:

```
# zpool autoreplace=on mpool
```

To simulate a bad device, I shut down the system and removed c5t4d0 from the system. The system now cannot contact the disk and has marked the removed disk as unavailable. With the system rebooted, you can examine the output of the `zpool status` command:

```
1    $ zpool status mpool
2    pool: mpool
3    state: DEGRADED
4    status: One or more devices could not be opened.  Sufficient replicas exist for
5    the pool to continue functioning in a degraded state.
6    action: Attach the missing device and online it using 'zpool online'.
7    see: http://www.sun.com/msg/ZFS-8000-2Q
8    scrub: resilver completed after 0h0m with 0 errors on Mon Apr  6 00:52:36 2009
9    config:
10
11   NAME           STATE     READ WRITE CKSUM
12   mpool          DEGRADED     0     0     0
13     mirror       ONLINE       0     0     0
14       c5t2d0     ONLINE       0     0     0
15       c5t3d0     ONLINE       0     0     0
16     mirror       DEGRADED     0     0     0
17       spare      DEGRADED     0     0     0
18         c5t4d0   UNAVAIL      0    89     0  cannot open
19         c5t14d0  ONLINE       0     0     0  31K resilvered
20       c5t5d0     ONLINE       0     0     0  31K resilvered
21   spares
22     c5t14d0      INUSE        currently in use
23
24   errors: No known data errors
```

On line 3, the state of the pool has been degraded, and line 4 tells you that the pool can continue in this state. On lines 6 and 7, ZFS tells you what actions you will need to take, and by going to the Web site, a more detailed message tells you how to correct the problem. Line 19 tells you that the spare disk has been resilvered with disk c5t5d0. Line 22 now gives you the new status of the spare disk c5t14d0.

The original definition of **resilver** is the process of restoring a glass mirror with a new silver backing. In ZFS, it is a re-creation of data by copying from one disk to another. In other volume management systems, the process is called **resynchronization**. Continuing the example, you can shut down the system and attach a new disk in the same location of the missing disk. The new disk at location c5t4d0 is automatically resilvered to the mirrored vdev, and the spare disk is put back to an available state.

```
$ zpool status mpool
pool: mpool
state: ONLINE
scrub: resilver completed after 0h0m with 0 errors on Mon Apr  6 02:21:05 2009
config:

NAME           STATE     READ WRITE CKSUM
mpool          ONLINE       0     0     0
  mirror       ONLINE       0     0     0
    c5t2d0     ONLINE       0     0     0
    c5t3d0     ONLINE       0     0     0
  mirror       ONLINE       0     0     0
    c5t4d0     ONLINE       0     0     0  23K resilvered
    c5t5d0     ONLINE       0     0     0  23K resilvered
  spares
    c5t14d0    AVAIL

errors: No known data errors
```

If the original disk is reattached to the system, ZFS does not handle this case with the same grace. Once the system is booted, the original disk must be detached from the ZFS pool. Next, the spare disk (c5d14d0) must be replaced with the original disk. The last step is to place the spare disk back into the spares group.

```
$ pfexec zpool detach mpool c5t4d0
$ pfexec zpool replace mpool c5t14d0 c5t4d0
$ pfexec zpool add mpool spare c5t14d0
$ zpool status mpool
pool: mpool
state: ONLINE
scrub: resilver completed after 0h0m with 0 errors on Mon Apr  6 02:50:25 2009
config:

NAME          STATE     READ WRITE CKSUM
mpool         ONLINE       0     0     0
  mirror      ONLINE       0     0     0
    c5t2d0    ONLINE       0     0     0
    c5t3d0    ONLINE       0     0     0
  mirror      ONLINE       0     0     0
    c5t4d0    ONLINE       0     0     0  40.5K resilvered
    c5t5d0    ONLINE       0     0     0  40.5K resilvered
spares
  c5t14d0     AVAIL

errors: No known data errors
```

2.8 Locating Disks for Replacement

Locating the correct disk for replacement is crucial. If the wrong disk is replaced, it could corrupt the whole ZFS pool. There is a simple process for locating a disk in an array using the `format` command. This technique works best when the disks are relatively quiet and have disk-access LEDs that can be seen while in operation.

If the disk is still accessible to Solaris, follow these steps:

1. Start the `format` command, and select the disk you want to locate by selecting the number before the drive.

2. Type **analyze**, and hit the Enter/Return key.

3. Select read test by typing **read**, and then hit Enter/Return.

4. Look at the array, and find the disk LED with constant access.

5. Once the disk is located, stop the read test by pressing Ctrl+C.

6. To exit the format utility, type **quit** and hit Return, and then type **quit** and hit Return again.

7. Replace the disk according to manufacturer's instructions.

If the damaged disk is not seen by `format`, try to light up the LEDs of the disks above and below the target number of the damaged disk. For example, if you were looking to find c5t6d0 and it was not seen by the `format` command, you would first locate c5t5d0 by using the format read test and then locate c5t7d0 by using the same method. The drive in between should be c5t6d0.

2.9 Example of a Misconfigured Pool

The following is an example of a ZFS pool that started as a RAID-Z pool and needed more space. The administrator just added the new disks to the pool. The status output follows.

```
$ zpool status -v
pool: mypool
state: ONLINE
status: One or more devices has experienced an error resulting in data
corruption.  Applications may be affected.
action: Restore the file in question if possible.  Otherwise restore the entire pool
from backup.
see: http://www.sun.com/msg/ZFS-8000-8A
scrub: resilver completed with 0 errors on Tue Nov 18 17:05:10 2008
config:

NAME          STATE     READ WRITE CKSUM
mypool        ONLINE       0     0    18
  raidz1      ONLINE       0     0     0
    c2t0d0    ONLINE       0     0     0
    c2t1d0    ONLINE       0     0     0
    c2t2d0    ONLINE       0     0     0
    c2t3d0    ONLINE       0     0     0
    c2t4d0    ONLINE       0     0     0
    c2t5d0    ONLINE       0     0     0
  c2t9d0      ONLINE       0     0     0
  c2t11d0     ONLINE       0     0     0
  c2t12d0     ONLINE       0     0    18
  c2t10d0     ONLINE       0     0     0
  c2t13d0     ONLINE       0     0     0
spares
  c2t8d0      AVAIL

errors: Permanent errors have been detected in the following files:

        mypool/dataset/u01:<0x2a07a>
        mypool/dataset/u01:<0x2da66>
```

c2t9d0, c2t10d0, c2t11d0, c2t12d0, and c2t13d0 are single-disk vdevs. They have no redundancy. The spare vdev will not help because there is nothing to resilver with when one of the single-disk vdevs fails. In this case, ZFS has detected permanent errors in mypool/dataset/u01 and has suggested an action of restoring the files from backup or restoring the whole pool from backup.

The ZFS pool is in danger of a single disk failure that may destroy the whole pool. The only way to get this pool to be redundant is to mirror all the single-vdev drives.

Figure 2.7 represents the ZFS pool mypool. The figure shows five single-disk vdevs with a single RAID-Z vdev. Any damage to the single disks will cause ZFS to lose data, or, worse, the pool will fail.

You can correct this configuration for pool redundancy in two ways:

- If there are enough disks, you can mirror the single-disk vdevs.
- You can back up all the file systems and re-create the pool. Then do a full restore of the file systems.

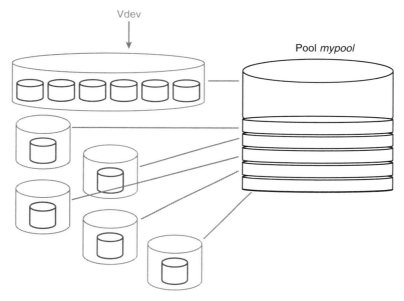

Figure 2.7 The ZFS pool *mypool* has a single RAID-Z vdev and five single-disk vdevs

The procedure to replace a single-disk vdev in the preceding example is to mirror the drive in question and then detach the bad drive. What follows is the command-line procedure:

1. Mirror the drive with bad sector problems:

   # **zpool replace mypool** <baddisk> <gooddisk>

2. Detach the bad disk:

   # **zpool detach mypool** <baddisk>

Installing and Booting a ZFS Root File System

This chapter describes how to install and boot a ZFS root file system and how to recover from a root pool disk failure. Upgrading and patching ZFS boot environments are also covered.

The capability to install and boot a ZFS root file system is available in the following Solaris releases:

- ***Solaris 10 10/08 release***: *The ZFS root file system is optional.*
- ***OpenSolaris 2008.11***: *The ZFS root file system is installed by default.*

3.1 Simplifying (Systems) Administration Using ZFS

ZFS installation and boot features simplify the administration process. Currently, ZFS file systems need a partition table prior to the installation of the Solaris OS. With traditional file systems, the following questions typically need to be answered:

- How large does the root (/) file system need to be?
- How large does /usr need to be?
- How large does the swap partition need to be?
- How large does the /var partition need to be?

- How much disk space needs to be allocated to use Solaris Live Upgrade?
- Will the current requirements change in 6 to 12 months?

With ZFS, answering the preceding questions at installation time is unnecessary.

In the past, a UNIX OS could be booted with just the root (/) file system, and disk reliability was not as good as today. By creating separate partitions, a system administrator could boot from the root (/) file system and repair a system with a few tools available in the root (/) file system. Today, it is not possible to boot without the /usr file system or directory.

In a ZFS boot environment, a separate /var file system is a good idea because you can set a quota so that if a runaway process exists or a denial-of-service attack occurs, the problem can be limited to that file system.

Disk partition sizes do not need to be decided at installation time when you use a ZFS root file system. Swap, dump, and boot environments can be dynamically allocated as needed. Swap and dump areas can be dynamically resized as requirements change. If more RAM is added to a system, swap and dump areas can be adjusted to accommodate new hardware.

Boot environments are managed by either Solaris Live Upgrade (Solaris 10) or the beadm command (OpenSolaris releases). The beadm command and the pkg commands simplify upgrading and patching the OpenSolaris releases. The advantages of using ZFS boot environments are as follows:

- Quick rollbacks
- Less downtime
- Quick cloning
- Safer patching
- Safer upgrades
- Simple administration

3.2 Installing a ZFS Root File System

Starting with the Solaris 10 10/08 release, a specialized installer provides the option to install a ZFS root file system. In addition, both the Solaris Live Upgrade and JumpStart installation methods support a ZFS root file system. The Solaris Live Upgrade feature enables an administrator to upgrade a system with minimal downtime, often just the time it takes to reboot. Should a problem arise that cannot be fixed quickly, the system can be rebooted to the previous state. JumpStart is a Solaris network installation facility that supports two modes: a normal install and a binary image install called Flash. Currently, Flash installation is not supported for ZFS. An unsupported workaround is provided at `http://blogs.sun.com/scottdickson/entry/a_much_better_way_to`.

A supported but limited ZFS and Flash solution should be available in an upcoming Solaris 10 release.

By default, the OpenSolaris release 2008.11 installs a ZFS root file system. No option exists for installing a UFS root file system.

3.2.1 ZFS Root File System Requirements

The following are the requirements for installing a ZFS root file system. Most of the requirements are the same as those for installing a Solaris release. The minimum requirement for disk space should be followed carefully.

- **Memory requirements**
  - 768MB RAM minimum
  - 1GB RAM recommended for better overall ZFS performance
- **Disk requirements**
  - 16GB is the minimum required to install a ZFS boot OS.
  - Maximum swap and dump sizes are based on physical memory and kernel needs at boot time but are generally sized no more than 2GB by the installation program.
  - The ZFS storage pool must be a nonredundant disk slice configuration or a mirrored disk slice configuration with the following characteristics:
    - There are no RAID-Z or RAID-Z2 vdevs and no separate log devices.
    - Disks must be labeled SMI.
    - Disks must be less than 1TB.
    - Disks on x86 systems must have an `fdisk` partition.
  - Compression can be enabled. The default is the `lzjb` algorithm. The `gzip` algorithm is also available, and compression is selectable.

3.2.2 ZFS Root Pool Recommendations

Review the following root pool recommendations:

- Use a mirrored root pool to reduce downtime due to hardware failures.
- Use one root pool for all data on small systems such as laptops and systems with two to four disks.

- Consider using one root pool and one nonroot pool for data management on larger systems where the performance of faster hardware is a factor in determining the best configuration.
- Use Solaris Live Upgrade to upgrade and patch ZFS boot environments.
- Keep root pool snapshots for recovery purposes.

3.2.3 Interactive ZFS Root File System Installation Example

The following example illustrates using a Solaris 10 10/08 x86 DVD to install a ZFS root file system. This example includes only the ZFS installation information.

1. Boot from the installation DVD or the network.
2. Select Solaris from the GRUB menu (see Figure 3.1).

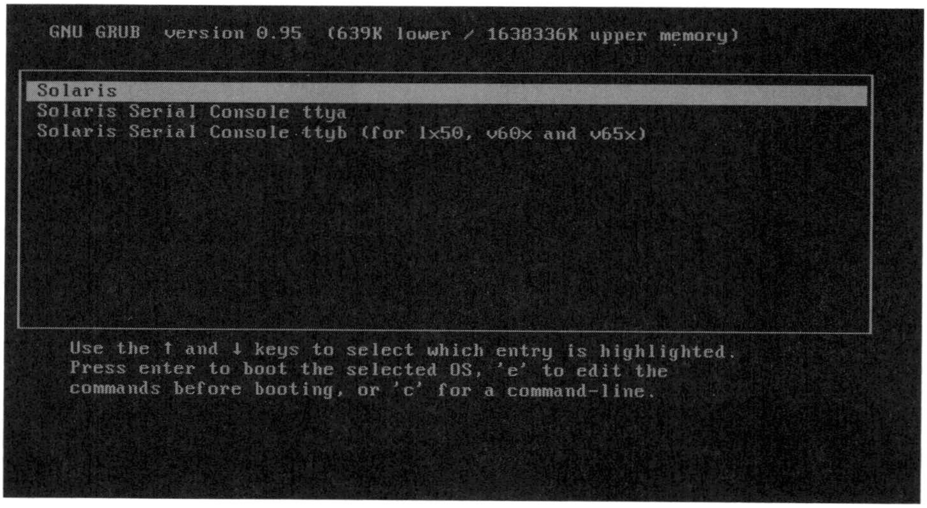

Figure 3.1 GRUB menu from DVD boot

3. Select the Solaris Interactive Text installation option from the menu, either selection 3 or 4 (see Figure 3.2).
4. Continue answering questions according to your environment.
5. Select ZFS as the root file system to be installed (see Figure 3.3).
6. In the form shown in Figure 3.4, adjust the size of the swap and dump devices, if necessary.
7. Select the /var partition on a separate dataset option.

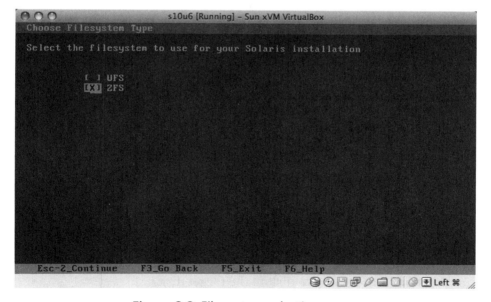

Figure 3.2 Solaris installation menu

Figure 3.3 File system selection menu

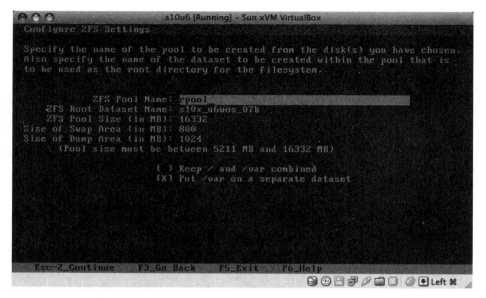

Figure 3.4 Form to adjust swap and dump devices and to select a separate /var partition

A separate /var partition is a best practice for security and backup/restore reasons. Separating /var and setting a quota on the dataset can limit denial-of-service attacks in which a rogue process fills the entire root disk, causing the system to crash. By excluding /var during backups, less data needs to be recorded and restored.

8. Continue with the installation.

3.3 Creating a Mirrored ZFS Root Configuration

You can create a mirrored ZFS root configuration by following these steps:

1. You can create a mirrored ZFS root pool in three basic steps after installation is complete. Alternatively, a mirrored root pool can be installed from a Jump-Start installation or during the initial installation process by selecting the disks to be components of the mirrored ZFS root pool. Copy the partition information from the source disk to the target disk.

   a. Label the disk as SMI. EFI labels are not supported for boot disks.

   ```
   # fdisk -B /dev/rdsk/c3d1p0
   ```

b. Partition the boot disk.

If the source and target disks are the same, use syntax similar to the following by substituting your disk devices:

prtvtoc /dev/rdsk/c3d0s2 | fmthard -s - /dev/rdsk/c3d1s2

If the source and target disks are different sizes, use the format command, and create a slice 0 from the end of the boot slice (usually 1/0/0) to the end of the disk.

2. Attach the new disk to the root pool:

zpool attach rpool c3d0s2 c3d1s2

3. After the new disk is resilvered and you can check the status with the zpool status command, install the boot block on the newly added disk:

installgrub /boot/grub/stage1 /boot/grub/stage2 /dev/rdsk/ c3d1s0

3.4 Testing a Mirrored ZFS Root Configuration

Testing a mirrored ZFS root configuration is important to ensure the configuration works before you really need to boot from the newly added disk. Follow these steps to test the configuration:

1. Shut down the system:

init 5

2. Remove or disconnect the primary boot disk.

3. Power on the system, and boot.

4. Log in to the system, and run the following command:

zpool status rpool

You will see output that looks like Figure 3.5.

5. Shut down the system.

6. Reconnect the primary boot disk.

7. Power on the system, and boot.

```
watanabe@opensolaris:~$ zpool status rpool
  pool: rpool
 state: DEGRADED
status: One or more devices could not be opened.  Sufficient replicas exist for
        the pool to continue functioning in a degraded state.
action: Attach the missing device and online it using 'zpool online'.
   see: http://www.sun.com/msg/ZFS-8000-2Q
 scrub: none requested
config:

        NAME        STATE     READ WRITE CKSUM
        rpool       DEGRADED     0     0     0
          mirror    DEGRADED     0     0     0
            c3d0s0  UNAVAIL      6 2.96K     0  cannot open
            c3d1s0  ONLINE       0     0     0

errors: No known data errors
watanabe@opensolaris:~$
```

Figure 3.5 Output of status of degraded pool *rpool*

3.5 Creating a Snapshot and Recovering a ZFS Root File System

A ZFS **snapshot** is a read-only copy of a file system. You can create and save snapshots of the ZFS root file system components for recovery in the event of a system failure.

Snapshot and recovery of the ZFS root file system should be planned and practiced. If you practice these steps in your environment, you will know approximately how much time it will take to perform a root file system recovery.

The examples in the following sections describe how to snapshot and recover from a local disk to save time and gain practice. Sending a snapshot to tape or to another server is preferred but can take more time.

3.5.1 Creating a Snapshot of the ZFS Root Storage Pool

The following steps describe how to create a pool for snapshots and then how to snapshot the root pool. Although this example uses the OpenSolaris ZFS boot environment, the steps are identical for the Solaris 10 release.

1. Create a storage pool for snapshots:

    # **zpool create -f bpool c5d29**

2. Create a ZFS file system in the snapshot pool:

    # **zfs create bpool/snap**

3. Create a directory for the OpenSolaris boot components:

    # **mkdir /bpool/snap/opensolaris**

4. Snapshot the root pool.

```
# zfs snapshot -r rpool@backup
# zfs list -t snapshot
NAME                                USED  AVAIL  REFER  MOUNTPOINT
rpool@backup                         17K      -    72K  -
rpool/ROOT@backup                      0      -    18K  -
rpool/ROOT/opensolaris@install      140M      -  2.21G  -
rpool/ROOT/opensolaris@backup      80.5M      -  2.35G  -
rpool/dump@backup                    16K      -   844M  -
rpool/export@backup                  15K      -    19K  -
rpool/export/home@backup             15K      -    19K  -
rpool/export/home/watanabe@backup   258K      -  22.4M  -
rpool/swap@backup                      0      -    16K  -
rzpool/export/home/watanabe@tx     95.8K      -  11.0M  -
```

3.5.2 Sending the ZFS Root Pool Snapshots to Storage

Sending root pool snapshots to storage can take some time to complete. Depending on disk, server, or network speeds, this process can consume a few hours. The following example shows how to send the snapshot to a different ZFS storage pool on the same system:

```
# zfs send -v rpool@backup > /bpool/snap/opensolaris/rpool.backup
# zfs send -vR rpool/ROOT/opensolaris@backup >
/bpool/snap/opensolaris/rpool.R.opensolaris.backup
sending from @ to rpool/ROOT/opensolaris@install
sending from @install to rpool/ROOT/opensolaris@backup
# zfs send -vR rpool/export/home@backup > /bpool/snap/opensolaris/export.backup
sending from @ to rpool/export/home@backup
sending from @ to rpool/export/home/watanabe@backup
```

3.5.3 Restoring the ZFS Root Pool Snapshots to a New Disk

Restoring root pool snapshots to a new disk is very straightforward. Practice these steps in your environment to learn approximately how much time it will take to restore from snapshots.

1. Boot from the installation DVD or the network.

2. Exit the installation program, and open a terminal window.

3. Import the snapshot pool:

   `# zpool -f import bpool`

4. Label the disk as SMI:

   `# fdisk -B /dev/rdsk/c3d1p0`

5. Partition the boot disk.

   Use the `format` command, and create a slice 0 from the end of the boot slice (usually 1/0/0) to the end of the disk.

6. Create a new directory to mount the restored root pool:

   # **mkdir /a**

7. Install the boot block on the root pool disk:

```
# installgrub /boot/grub/stage1 /boot/grub/stage2
/dev/rdsk/c3d1s0
```

8. Create the new root pool to restore the snapshots:

```
# zpool create -f -o failmode=continue -R /a -m
legacy -o cachefile=/etc/zfs/zpool.cache rpool c3d1s0
```

9. Receive each snapshot in order from the top level:

```
# cat /bpool/snap/opensolaris/rpool.backup | zfs
receive -dvF rpool
# cat /bpool/snap/opensolaris/rpool.R.opensolaris.backup| zfs receive -dvF rpool
# cat /bpool/snap/opensolaris/export.backup| zfs
receive -dvF rpool
```

10. Set the `bootfs` property on the root pool:

    # **zpool set bootfs=rpool/ROOT/opensolaris rpool**

11. Create a 2GB dump device:

    # **zfs create -V 2G rpool/dump**

12. Create a 2GB swap device with a 4KB block size:

    # **zfs create -V 2G -b 4k rpool/swap**

13. Reboot the system with the new disk:

    # **init 6**

3.6 Managing ZFS Boot Environments with Solaris Live Upgrade

You can use Solaris Live Upgrade to manage boot environments in the Solaris 10 release. Solaris Live Upgrade copies the current operating environment, and then you can apply an OS upgrade or a patch cluster to this boot environment. Once the upgrade process is completed, the new boot environment is activated and booted with minimal downtime. You can roll back to the previous environment by activating the previous boot environment and rebooting. Starting in the Solaris 10 10/08 release, you can use Solaris Live Upgrade to migrate a UFS root file system to a ZFS root file system.

3.6.1 Migrating a UFS Root File System to a ZFS Root File System

The following procedure describes how to migrate to a ZFS root file system by using Solaris Live Upgrade. The one-way migration is supported for the UFS root file system components only. To migrate nonroot UFS file systems, use the `ufsdump` and `ufsrestore` commands to copy UFS data and restore the data into a ZFS file system.

The ZFS root file system migration involves three major steps:

1. Preparing the disk and creating a ZFS storage pool
2. Creating a new ZFS boot environment
3. Activating the ZFS boot environment

The following example uses a UFS root file system on an x86-based system. The primary disk is c0d0s0, and the target update disk is c0d1.

1. With the disk labeled as SMI, create a new `s0` partition and a new ZFS pool:

```
bash-3.00# fdisk -B /dev/rdsk/c0d1p0
bash-3.00# format
Searching for disks...done


AVAILABLE DISK SELECTIONS:
       0. c0d0 <DEFAULT cyl 2085 alt 2 hd 255 sec 63>
          /pci@0,0/pci-ide@1,1/ide@0/cmdk@0,0
       1. c0d1 <DEFAULT cyl 2085 alt 2 hd 255 sec 63>
          /pci@0,0/pci-ide@1,1/ide@0/cmdk@1,0
Specify disk (enter its number): 1
selecting c0d1
```

continues

```
Controller working list found
[disk formatted, defect list found]


FORMAT MENU:
        disk       - select a disk
        type       - select (define) a disk type
        partition  - select (define) a partition table
        current    - describe the current disk
        format     - format and analyze the disk
        fdisk      - run the fdisk program
        repair     - repair a defective sector
        show       - translate a disk address
        label      - write label to the disk
        analyze    - surface analysis
        defect     - defect list management
        backup     - search for backup labels
        verify     - read and display labels
        save       - save new disk/partition definitions
        volname    - set 8-character volume name
        !<cmd>     - execute <cmd>, then return
        quit
format> p


PARTITION MENU:
        0        - change `0' partition
        1        - change `1' partition
        2        - change `2' partition
        3        - change `3' partition
        4        - change `4' partition
        5        - change `5' partition
        6        - change `6' partition
        7        - change `7' partition
        select - select a predefined table
        modify - modify a predefined partition table
        name   - name the current table
        print  - display the current table
        label  - write partition map and label to the disk
        !<cmd> - execute <cmd>, then return
        quit
partition> p
Current partition table (original):
Total disk cylinders available: 2085 + 2 (reserved cylinders)

Part      Tag    Flag  Cylinders    Size            Blocks
  0 unassigned   wm    0            0        (0/0/0)           0
  1 unassigned   wm    0            0        (0/0/0)           0
  2     backup   wu    0 - 2084 15.97GB      (2085/0/0) 33495525
  3 unassigned   wm    0            0        (0/0/0)           0
  4 unassigned   wm    0            0        (0/0/0)           0
  5 unassigned   wm    0            0        (0/0/0)           0
  6 unassigned   wm    0            0        (0/0/0)           0
  7 unassigned   wm    0            0        (0/0/0)           0
  8       boot   wu    0 - 0    7.84MB       (1/0/0)       16065
  9 alternates   wm    1 - 2   15.69MB       (2/0/0)       32130

partition> 0
Part      Tag    Flag  Cylinders    Size            Blocks
  0 unassigned   wm    0            0        (0/0/0)           0

 Enter partition id tag[unassigned]: root
 Enter partition permission flags[wm]:
 Enter new starting cyl[3]:
```

continues

```
Enter partition size[0b, 0c, 3e, 0.00mb, 0.00gb]: 2082c
partition> p
Current partition table (unnamed):
Total disk cylinders available: 2085 + 2 (reserved cylinders)

Part      Tag   Flag  Cylinders    Size              Blocks
  0       root   wm    3 - 2084   15.95GB   (2082/0/0) 33447330
  1 unassigned   wm    0            0       (0/0/0)           0
  2     backup   wu    0 - 2084   15.97GB   (2085/0/0) 33495525
  3 unassigned   wm    0            0       (0/0/0)           0
  4 unassigned   wm    0            0       (0/0/0)           0
  5 unassigned   wm    0            0       (0/0/0)           0
  6 unassigned   wm    0            0       (0/0/0)           0
  7 unassigned   wm    0            0       (0/0/0)           0
  8       boot   wu    0 -    0    7.84MB   (1/0/0)       16065
  9 alternates   wm    1 -    2   15.69MB   (2/0/0)       32130

partition> label
Ready to label disk, continue? y

partition> q

FORMAT MENU:
      disk      - select a disk
      type      - select (define) a disk type
      partition - select (define) a partition table
      current   - describe the current disk
      format    - format and analyze the disk
      fdisk     - run the fdisk program
      repair    - repair a defective sector
      show      - translate a disk address
      label     - write label to the disk
      analyze   - surface analysis
      defect    - defect list management
      backup    - search for backup labels
      verify    - read and display labels
      save      - save new disk/partition definitions
      volname   - set 8-character volume name
      !<cmd>    - execute <cmd>, then return
      quit
format> l
      Ready to label disk, continue? y
format> q
```

2. Create a new ZFS storage pool called rpool:

   bash-3.00# **zpool create rpool c0d1s0**

3. Create a new ZFS boot environment.

```
bash-3.00# lucreate -n 10u6be-zfs -p rpool
Checking GRUB menu...
Analyzing system configuration.
No name for current boot environment.
INFORMATION: The current boot environment is not named -
assigning name <c0d0s0>.
Current boot environment is named <c0d0s0>.
Creating initial configuration for primary boot environment <c0d0s0>.
The device </dev/dsk/c0d0s0> is not a root device for any
boot environment; cannot get BE ID.
PBE configuration successful: PBE name <c0d0s0> PBE Boot
Device </dev/dsk/c0d0s0>.
```

continues

```
Comparing source boot environment <c0d0s0> file systems with
the file system(s) you specified for the new boot environment. Determining which
file systems should be in the new boot environment.
Updating boot environment description database on all BEs.
Updating system configuration files.
The device </dev/dsk/c0d1s0> is not a root device for any boot environment;
cannot get BE ID.
Creating configuration for boot environment <10u6be-zfs>.
Source boot environment is <c0d0s0>.
Creating boot environment <10u6be-zfs>.
Creating file systems on boot environment <10u6be-zfs>.
Creating <zfs> file system for </> in zone <global> on <rpool/ROOT/10u6be-zfs>.
Populating file systems on boot environment <10u6be-zfs>.
Checking selection integrity.
Integrity check OK.
Populating contents of mount point </>.
Copying.
Creating shared file system mount points.
Creating compare databases for boot environment <10u6be-zfs>.
Creating compare database for file system </rpool/ROOT>.
Creating compare database for file system </>.
Updating compare databases on boot environment <10u6be-zfs>.
Making boot environment <10u6be-zfs> bootable.
Updating bootenv.rc on ABE <10u6be-zfs>.
File </boot/grub/menu.lst> propagation successful
Copied GRUB menu from PBE to ABE
No entry for BE <10u6be-zfs> in GRUB menu
Population of boot environment <10u6be-zfs> successful.
Creation of boot environment <10u6be-zfs> successful.
bash-3.00# lustatus
Boot Environment      Is        Active Active   Can    Copy
Name                  Complete  Now    On Reboot Delete Status
-------------------- --------- ------ --------- ------ -------
c0d0s0                yes       yes    yes       no     -
10u6be-zfs            yes       no     no        yes    -
bash-3.00# zfs list
NAME                    USED   AVAIL  REFER  MOUNTPOINT
rpool                   4.93G  10.7G   24K   /rpool
rpool/ROOT              3.92G  10.7G   18K   /rpool/ROOT
rpool/ROOT/10u6be-zfs   3.92G  10.7G  3.92G  /
rpool/dump              518M   11.2G   16K   -
rpool/swap              518M   11.2G   16K   -
```

4. Activate the new ZFS boot environment:

```
bash-3.00# luactivate -n 10u6be-zfs
Generating boot-sign, partition and slice information for PBE <c0d0s0>
A Live Upgrade Sync operation will be performed on startup of boot
environment <10u6be-zfs>.

Generating boot-sign for ABE <10u6be-zfs>
NOTE: File </etc/bootsign> not found in top level dataset for BE <10u6be-zfs>
Generating partition and slice information for ABE <10u6be-zfs>
Boot menu exists.
Generating multiboot menu entries for PBE.
Generating multiboot menu entries for ABE.
Disabling splashimage
Re-enabling splashimage
```

continues

```
No more bootadm entries. Deletion of bootadm entries is complete.
GRUB menu default setting is unaffected
Done eliding bootadm entries.

*************************************************************

The target boot environment has been activated. It will be used when you reboot.
NOTE: You MUST NOT USE the reboot, halt, or uadmin commands. You MUST USE either the
init or the shutdown command when you reboot. If you do not use either init or shutdown,
the system will not boot using the target BE.

*************************************************************

In case of a failure while booting to the target BE, the
following process needs to be followed to fallback to the currently working
boot environment:

1. Boot from the Solaris failsafe or boot in Single User mode from Solaris
Install CD or Network.

2. Mount the Parent boot environment root slice to some
directory (like /mnt). You can use the following command to mount:

    mount -Fufs /dev/dsk/c0d0s0 /mnt

3. Run <luactivate> utility without any arguments from the Parent boot
environment root slice, as shown below:

    /mnt/sbin/luactivate

4. luactivate, activates the previous working boot environment and
indicates the result.

5. Exit Single User mode and reboot the machine.

*************************************************************

Modifying boot archive service
Propagating findroot GRUB for menu conversion.
File </etc/lu/installgrub.findroot> propagation successful
File </etc/lu/stage1.findroot> propagation successful
File </etc/lu/stage2.findroot> propagation successful
File </etc/lu/GRUB_capability> propagation successful
Deleting stale GRUB loader from all BEs.
File </etc/lu/installgrub.latest> deletion successful
File </etc/lu/stage1.latest> deletion successful
File </etc/lu/stage2.latest> deletion successful
Activation of boot environment <10u6be-zfs> successful.
bash-3.00# lustatus
Boot Environment      Is          Active Active   Can     Copy
Name                  Complete    Now    On Reboot Delete  Status
------------------    --------    ------ --------- ------  -------
c0d0s0                yes         yes    no        no      -
10u6be-zfs            yes         no     yes       no      -
bash-3.00# init 6
updating /platform/i86pc/boot_archive
propagating updated GRUB menu
Saving existing file </boot/grub/menu.lst> in top level dataset
for BE <10u6be-zfs> as <mount-point>//boot/grub/menu.lst.prev.
File </boot/grub/menu.lst> propagation successful
File </etc/lu/GRUB_backup_menu> propagation successful
File </etc/lu/menu.cksum> propagation successful
File </sbin/bootadm> propagation successful
```

Notice the difference in the `lustatus` output. After the `luactivate` operation, the Active On Reboot flag changed for boot environment 10u6be-zfs.

3.6.2 Patching a ZFS Boot Environment with Solaris Live Upgrade

Patching a boot environment by using Solaris Live Upgrade minimizes downtime and is a simpler and safer way to patch a system. Any patching has risks of not working or making a system unbootable. You can also use Solaris Live Upgrade to add new packages or upgrade a system to a new release level.

After a patch is applied, the new boot environment can be booted. If any problems occur, the system can be rebooted to the original boot environment.

To patch a ZFS boot environment with Solaris Live Upgrade, follow these steps:

1. Create a new boot environment to be patched:

```
bash-3.00# lucreate -n 10u6be-1
Checking GRUB menu...
System has findroot enabled GRUB
Analyzing system configuration.
Comparing source boot environment <10u6be-zfs> file
systems with the file
system(s) you specified for the new boot environment.
Determining which
file systems should be in the new boot environment.
Updating boot environment description database on all BEs.
Updating system configuration files.
Creating configuration for boot environment <10u6be-1>.
Source boot environment is <10u6be-zfs>.
Creating boot environment <10u6be-1>.
Cloning file systems from boot environment <10u6be-zfs> to
create boot
environment <10u6be-1>.
Creating snapshot for <rpool/ROOT/10u6be-zfs> on
<rpool/ROOT/10u6be-zfs@10u6be-1>.
Creating clone for <rpool/ROOT/10u6be-zfs@10u6be-1> on
<rpool/ROOT/10u6be-1>.
Setting canmount=noauto for </> in zone <global> on
<rpool/ROOT/10u6be-1>.
Saving existing file </boot/grub/menu.lst> in top level
dataset for BE
<10u6be-1> as <mount-point>//boot/grub/menu.lst.prev.
File </boot/grub/menu.lst> propagation successful
Copied GRUB menu from PBE to ABE
No entry for BE <10u6be-1> in GRUB menu
Population of boot environment <10u6be-1> successful.
Creation of boot environment <10u6be-1> successful.
```

2. Unpack the downloaded patch cluster to the `/var/tmp` directory:

```
bash-3.00# unzip 10_x86_Recommended.zip
```

3. Upgrade the new ZFS boot environment:

```
bash-3.00# luupgrade -t  -n 10u6be-1 -s /var/tmp/10_x86_Recommended

System has findroot enabled GRUB
No entry for BE <10u6be-1> in GRUB menu
Validating the contents of the media
</var/tmp/10_x86_Recommended>.
The media contains 148 software patches that can be added.
All 148 patches will be added because you did not specify
any specific patches to add.
Mounting the BE <10u6be-1>.
Adding patches to the BE <10u6be-1>.
Validating patches...

Loading patches installed on the system...

Done!

Loading patches requested to install.

...Deleted Output…

Unmounting the BE <10u6be-1>.
The patch add to the BE <10u6be-1> completed.
```

4. Activate the new ZFS boot environment:

```
bash-3.00# luactivate -n 10u6be-1
System has findroot enabled GRUB
Generating boot-sign, partition and slice information for
PBE <10u6be-zfs>
A Live Upgrade Sync operation will be performed on startup
of boot
environment <10u6be-1>.

Generating boot-sign for ABE <10u6be-1>
Saving existing file </etc/bootsign> in top level dataset for BE
<10u6be-1> as <mount-point>//etc/bootsign.prev.
Generating partition and slice information for ABE <10u6be-1>
Copied boot menu from top level dataset.
Generating multiboot menu entries for PBE.
Generating multiboot menu entries for ABE.
Disabling splashimage
Re-enabling splashimage
No more bootadm entries. Deletion of bootadm entries is complete.
GRUB menu default setting is unaffected
Done eliding bootadm entries.

*****************************************************************

The target boot environment has been activated. It will be used when you reboot.
NOTE: You MUST NOT USE the reboot, halt, or uadmin commands. You MUST USE either the
init or the shutdown command when you reboot. If you do not use either init or shutdown,
the system will not boot using the target BE.

*****************************************************************
```

continues

```
In case of a failure while booting to the target BE, the following process needs
to be followed to fallback to the currently working boot environment:

1. Boot from Solaris failsafe or boot in single user mode from the Solaris Install
CD or Network.

2. Mount the Parent boot environment root slice to some directory (like /mnt).
You can use the following command to mount:

    mount -Fzfs /dev/dsk/c0d1s0 /mnt

3. Run <luactivate> utility without any arguments from the Parent boot
environment root slice, as shown below:

    /mnt/sbin/luactivate

4. luactivate, activates the previous working boot environment and
indicates the result.

5. Exit Single User mode and reboot the machine.

**************************************************************

Modifying boot archive service
Propagating findroot GRUB for menu conversion.
File </etc/lu/installgrub.findroot> propagation successful
File </etc/lu/stage1.findroot> propagation successful
File </etc/lu/stage2.findroot> propagation successful
File </etc/lu/GRUB_capability> propagation successful
Deleting stale GRUB loader from all BEs.
File </etc/lu/installgrub.latest> deletion successful
File </etc/lu/stage1.latest> deletion successful
File </etc/lu/stage2.latest> deletion successful
Activation of boot environment <10u6be-1> successful.
```

5. Check the status of the Active On Reboot flag for the new ZFS boot
   environment:

```
bash-3.00# lustatus
Boot Environment    Is        Active Active    Can    Copy
Name                Complete  Now    On Reboot Delete Status
------------------  --------  ------ --------- ------ -------
c0d0s0              yes       no     no        yes    -
10u6be-zfs          yes       yes    no        no     -
10u6be-1            yes       no     yes       no     -
```

6. Shut down the system:

```
bash-3.00# init 0
updating /platform/i86pc/boot_archive
propagating updated GRUB menu
Saving existing file </boot/grub/menu.lst> in top level
dataset for BE
<10u6be-1> as <mount-point>//boot/grub/menu.lst.prev.
File </boot/grub/menu.lst> propagation successful
File </etc/lu/GRUB_backup_menu> propagation successful
File </etc/lu/menu.cksum> propagation successful
File </sbin/bootadm> propagation successful
```

3.7 Managing ZFS Boot Environments (`beadm`)

Managing ZFS boot environments with the `beadm` command simplifies upgrades and rollbacks. The basic features of the `beadm` command enable you to create a boot environment, activate a boot environment, and destroy a boot environment.

You can use the `beadm` and `pkg` commands to update an OpenSolaris release to a current build. Use caution when upgrading to a new development build. These builds are not as well tested as the release candidates and are unsupported. Using the `beadm` command to manage and upgrade your boot environments can reduce risk by enabling you to revert to the prior boot environment.

3.8 Upgrading a ZFS Boot Environment (`beadm`)

Upgrade a ZFS boot environment using `beadm` by following these steps:

1. Create a new boot environment named opensolaris1:

   ```
   $ pfexec beadm create opensolaris1
   ```

2. Mount the new boot environment. For example, mount the new boot environment at /mnt:

   ```
   $ pfexec beadm mount opensolaris1 /mnt
   $ pfexec beadm list
   BE           Active Mountpoint Space Policy Created
   --           ------ ---------- ----- ------ -------
   opensolaris  NR     /          2.38G static 2009-01-29 23:32
   opensolaris1 -      /mnt       64.0K static 2009-01-30 01:43
   Set pkg repository to OpenSolaris development
   ```

3. Set the `pkg` authority to the OpenSolaris development repository:

   ```
   $ pfexec pkg set-authority -P -O http://pkg.opensolaris.org/dev opensolaris.org
   $ pfexec pkg authority
   AUTHORITY               URL
   opensolaris.org (preferred)  http://pkg.opensolaris.org/dev/
   ```

4. Update the image of the new boot environment:

   ```
   $ pfexec pkg -R /mnt image-update -v
   ```

5. Activate the new boot environment.

    After activating the `opensolaris1` boot environment, the Active On Reboot flag `R` has moved (line 12). The current active boot environment flag is represented by `N`.

```
1   $ beadm list
2   BE            Active Mountpoint Space  Policy Created
3   --            ------ ---------- ----- ------ -------
4   opensolaris   NR     /                2.46G static 2009-01-29 23:32
5   opensolaris1  -      /mnt             1.41G static 2009-01-30 01:43
6   watanabe@opensolaris:~$
7   $ pfexec beadm activate opensolaris1
8   $ beadm list
9   BE            Active Mountpoint Space  Policy Created
10  --            ------ ---------- ----- ------ -------
11  opensolaris   N      /                68.50M static 2009-01-29 23:32
12  opensolaris1  R      /mnt             3.80G  static 2009-01-30 01:43
```

6. Reboot the system:
    ```
    $ pfexec init 6
    ```

7. Log in and verify the new image.

    In the following example, the new boot environment is at build 105:

```
$ cat /etc/release
                  OpenSolaris 2009.04 snv_105 X86
       Copyright 2009 Sun Microsystems, Inc.  All Rights Reserved.
                   Use is subject to license terms.
                    Assembled 22 December 2008
$ beadm list
BE            Active Mountpoint Space  Policy Created
--            ------ ---------- ----- ------ -------
opensolaris   -      -                122.34M static 2009-01-29 23:32
opensolaris1  NR     /                3.95G   static 2009-01-30 01:43
```

3.9 Upgrading a ZFS Boot Environment (`pkg`)

The OpenSolaris release has made upgrades easier to do. The `pkg image-update` command creates a boot environment and upgrades and activates it without the `-R` flag. Follow these steps to upgrade a ZFS boot using `pkg`:

1. Set the `pkg` authority to the OpenSolaris development repository:
    ```
    $ pfexec pkg set-authority -P -O http://pkg.opensolaris.org/dev
    opensolaris.org
    ```

2. Update the image of the new boot environment.

    The `pkg` command creates a new boot environment by using the current name and appending a number to it:

```
$ pfexec  pkg image-update -v
... Deleted output ...
$ beadm list
BE              Active Mountpoint Space   Policy Created
--              ------ ---------- -----   ------ -------
opensolaris     N      /          17.37M  static 2009-01-29 23:32
opensolaris-1   R      -          4.04G   static 2009-01-30 06:24
opensolaris1    -      -          1.50G   static 2009-01-30 01:43
```

    Figure 3.6 shows the verbose output of the image update.

```
pkg:/SUNWxdg-user-dirs-gtk@0.5.11,5.11-0.101:20081119T231321Z -> pkg:/SUNWxdg-us
er-dirs-gtk@0.5.11,5.11-0.105:20090108T204720Z
pkg:/SUNWipoib@0.5.11,5.11-0.101:20081119T223459Z -> pkg:/SUNWipoib@0.5.11,5.11-
0.105:20090108T202904Z
Actuators:
        restart_fmri: svc:/system/manifest-import:default
        restart_fmri: svc:/application/desktop-cache/input-method-cache:default
        restart_fmri: svc:/application/desktop-cache/icon-cache:default
        restart_fmri: svc:/application/desktop-cache/pixbuf-loaders-installer:defa
ult
        restart_fmri: svc:/application/desktop-cache/gconf-cache:default
        restart_fmri: svc:/system/manifest-import:default
        restart_fmri: svc:/application/desktop-cache/icon-cache:default
None
PHASE                                     ITEMS
Indexing Packages                        554/554
DOWNLOAD                            PKGS        FILES      XFER (MB)
Completed                          556/556   9515/9515 294.22/294.22

PHASE                                    ACTIONS
Removal Phase                          5248/5248
Install Phase                          3878/3878
Update Phase                          14264/14264
Reading Existing Index                    9/9
```

Figure 3.6 Verbose output of the image update

3. Reboot to the new boot environment:

    ```
    $ pfexec init 6
    ```

3.10 References

You can find more information at the following locations:

- **Solaris ZFS Administration Guide**:
  `http://docs.sun.com/app/docs/doc/819-5461`
- **ZFS Best Practices Guide**:
  `www.solarisinternals.com/wiki/index.php/ZFS_Best_Practices_`
  `Guide`
- **ZFS Troubleshooting Guide**:
  `www.solarisinternals.com/wiki/index.php/ZFS_Troubleshooting_`
  `Guide`

4

Managing ZFS Home Directories

This chapter describes how to use ZFS file systems for users' home directories. Managing home directories with ZFS is very easy:

- *Quotas and reservations are easier to manage than in other file systems.*
- *Individual users can recover their own files from snapshots, leaving the administrator to do other work.*
- *Compression on file systems enables better disk management.*
- *File system properties can be assigned depending on users' needs.*

4.1 Managing Quotas and Reservations on ZFS File Systems

Quotas and reservations are storage management tools that control the maximum and minimum that a file system can consume from a storage pool. Using a file system per user, you can control the storage resources each user can consume. This is a different model from what traditional UNIX operating systems have used in the past, where the user ID was used to aggregate the consumption of storage blocks. ZFS is much simpler to administer, because you can create file systems to aggregate the consumption by user.

A best practice is to set up each user or project with its own ZFS file system, which creates a nice, granular storage management practice. Depending on a user's needs, you can set up different ZFS properties on specific home directory file systems, if required.

Another good management practice for a server is to separate the system root pool data from any data pools or file systems. Even if a mistake is made with the root pool, the data can be recovered easily.

4.1.1 Setting the `quota` and `refquota` Properties

`quota` and `refquota` are two ZFS properties that control the maximum consumption of storage blocks per file system. `quota` is the absolute maximum that a file system can consume, including descendents, snapshots, and clones. `refquota` limits only the file system, not including descendents, snapshots, and clones.

4.1.1.1 Using the `quota` Setting

The most basic case is setting a quota on a user's home directory as a ZFS file system. In this example, a simple quota is set on user layne's home directory, and he attempts to write to the file system:

```
1   $ zfs list homepool/export/home/layne
2   NAME                         USED  AVAIL  REFER MOUNTPOINT
3   homepool/export/home/layne  8.18M   572M  8.18M /export/home/layne
4   $ pfexec zfs set quota=20m homepool/export/home/layne
5   $ zfs list homepool/export/home/layne
6   NAME                         USED  AVAIL  REFER MOUNTPOINT
7   homepool/export/home/layne  8.18M  11.8M  8.18M /export/home/layne
```

On line 3, the availability is 572MB. After setting the quota on line 4 to 20MB, the available storage to user layne drops to 11.8MB.

Next, user layne adds files to the home directory until the quota limit is hit:

```
1    layne@opensolaris:~$ mkfile 2m testfile1;mkfile 2m testfile2
2    layne@opensolaris:~$ mkfile 2m testfile3;mkfile 2m testfile4; mkfile 2m testfile5
3    layne@opensolaris:~$ mkfile 2m testfile6
4    testfile6: initialized 1835008 of 2097152 bytes: Disc quota exceeded
5    layne@opensolaris:~$ ls -lF test*
6    -rw------- 1 layne other 2097152 2009-02-12 07:47 testfile1
7    -rw------- 1 layne other 2097152 2009-02-12 07:47 testfile2
8    -rw------- 1 layne other 2097152 2009-02-12 07:47 testfile3
9    -rw------- 1 layne other 2097152 2009-02-12 07:48 testfile4
10   -rw------- 1 layne other 2097152 2009-02-12 07:48 testfile5
11   -rw------- 1 layne other 2097152 2009-02-12 07:48 testfile6
12   layne@opensolaris:~$ du -sh test*
13   2.1M      testfile1
14   2.1M      testfile2
15   2.1M      testfile3
16   2.1M      testfile4
17   2.1M      testfile5
18   1.9M      testfile6
19   layne@opensolaris:~$ touch testfile5
20   touch: setting times of `testfile5': Disc quota exceeded
21   layne@opensolaris:~$ rm testfile6
22   layne@opensolaris:~$
```

The write fails on line 4 with only 1,835,008 bytes written to disk. The `ls` output shows that `testfile6` is the same size as the rest of the 2MB files written. The size difference is because of the way that `ls` calculates the size of the file. The `ls` command determines file size by using the difference between the first and last blocks of the file. To get a more accurate size, the `du` command is used.

On line 20, the `touch` fails because of the copy-on-write (COW) feature of ZFS. Because ZFS would need to copy the file first and no available space exists, the write fails. Deleting the file `testfile6` is no problem, because ZFS does not have to keep a copy.

ZFS does not write in place like most other file systems. Instead, it will write a new copy of the data and move the pointers to the data once the operation is complete via COW.

Next, the following example re-creates `testfile6` and takes a snapshot of the file system that is full:

```
1    layne@opensolaris:~$ mkfile 2m testfile6
2    testfile6: initialized 1835008 of 2097152 bytes: Disc quota exceeded
3    <zfs snapshot taken here>
4    layne@opensolaris:~$ touch testfile6
5    touch: setting times of `testfile6': Disc quota exceeded
6    layne@opensolaris:~$ rm testfile6
7    rm: cannot remove `testfile6': Disc quota exceeded
```

Again, the `touch` file on line 5 fails. On line 7, the file cannot be removed because the snapshot needs more room to rewrite the blocks to point to the snapshot, but the quota is a hard limit.

You can correct this problem in four ways:

- Destroy the snapshot.
- Increase the quota.
- Remove the quota.
- Use `refquota` to keep the usage exclusive to the file system and to 20MB.

4.1.1.2 Using the `refquota` Setting

Using the `refquota` setting limits the storage used in just the normal file system. The setting has no effect on any descendents, snapshots, or clones. In this case, any snapshots or clones are not counted against the quota limits of the user's home directory. The following example illustrates how to set `refquota` to 20MB and then attempts to write files to the `refquota` limit.

First, clear out the previous quota and remove the test files for user layne. On line 1, you remove the snapshot called *samplesnap*, and next you clear the quota set in the previous example. On line 3, you retrieve the `quota` and `refquota` values to make sure they are reset to the defaults.

```
1   $ pfexec zfs destroy homepool/export/home/layne@samplesnap
2   $ pfexec zfs quota=none homepool/export/home/layne
3   $ zfs get quota,refquota homepool/export/home/layne
4   NAME                           PROPERTY  VALUE    SOURCE
5   homepool/export/home/layne     quota     none     default
6   homepool/export/home/layne     refquota  none     default
```

Remove old test files:

layne@opensolaris:~$ **rm test***

Next, set the `refquota` setting to 20MB for user layne, and check the settings by issuing the `zfs get` command on line 2:

```
1   $ pfexec zfs refquota=20m homepool/export/home/layne
2   $ zfs get quota,refquota homepool/export/home/layne
3   NAME                           PROPERTY  VALUE    SOURCE
4   homepool/export/home/layne     quota     none     default
5   homepool/export/home/layne     refquota  20M      local
```

Create a couple of 10MB files until the `refquota` limit is reached and an error message is generated by the system. The output of the `ls` command leads you to believe that both files are the same size, but the output of the `du` command tells a different story. The `du` command counts blocks used and is accurate concerning the size of the file.

```
layne@opensolaris:~$ mkfile 10m testfile1
layne@opensolaris:~$ mkfile 10m testfile2
testfile2: initialized 1835008 of 10485760 bytes: Disc quota exceeded
layne@opensolaris:~$ ls -lF test*
-rw------- 1 layne other 10485760 2009-02-12 15:57 testfile1
-rw------- 1 layne other 10485760 2009-02-12 15:57 testfile2
layne@opensolaris:~$ du -h test*
10M     testfile1
1.9M    testfile2
```

Next, take a snapshot of the home directory:

$ **pfexec zfs snapshot homepool/export/home/layne@samplesnap**

Remove a test file, and check the storage usage:

```
1   layne@opensolaris:~$ zfs list homepool/export/home/layne
2   NAME                          USED   AVAIL  REFER  MOUNTPOINT
3   homepool/export/home/layne    20.1M      0  20.1M  /export/home/layne
4   layne@opensolaris:~$ rm testfile2
5   layne@opensolaris:~$ zfs list homepool/export/home/layne
6   NAME                          USED   AVAIL  REFER  MOUNTPOINT
7   homepool/export/home/layne    20.1M  1.82M  18.2M  /export/home/layne
```

On line 3, 0 bytes are available for use in layne's home directory. After removing `testfile2`, 1.82MB is available. Notice also that the used storage has not changed because the file `testfile2` is still in the snapshot.

Using a `refquota` property, the file system continues to grow until the `refquota` limit is reached. A file system with a `refquota` set means that space that is consumed by descendents can grow until a parent file system quota is reached or the pool's available capacity is reached.

4.1.1.3 Limiting the Storage Size of Descendents

You can limit the storage size of file system descendent data by using the `quota` setting. If you wanted to limit the home directories of all users to 250MB, set the quota in the parent directory, for example, `homepool/export/home`, for all user home directories:

```
1   $ zfs list
2   NAME                            USED   AVAIL  REFER  MOUNTPOINT
3   homepool                        108M   560M   26.9K  /homepool
4   homepool/export                 107M   560M   28.4K  /export
5   homepool/export/home            107M   560M   50.9K  /export/home
6   homepool/export/home/ken        8.17M  560M   8.17M  /export/home/ken
7   homepool/export/home/layne      20.1M  1.82M  18.2M  /export/home/layne
8   homepool/export/home/watanabe   78.8M  560M   71.2M  /export/home/watanabe
...Output delete...
9   $ pfexec zfs quota=250m homepool/export/home
10  $ zfs get quota homepool/export/home
11  NAME                      PROPERTY  VALUE  SOURCE
12  homepool/export/home      quota     250M   local
13  $ zfs list
14  NAME                            USED   AVAIL  REFER  MOUNTPOINT
15  homepool                        108M   560M   26.9K  /homepool
16  homepool/export                 107M   560M   28.4K  /export
17  homepool/export/home            107M   143M   50.9K  /export/home
18  homepool/export/home/ken        8.17M  143M   8.17M  /export/home/ken
19  homepool/export/home/layne      20.1M  1.82M  18.2M  /export/home/layne
20  homepool/export/home/watanabe   78.8M  143M   71.2M  /export/home/watanabe
...Output deleted...
```

After setting a quota of 250MB on `homepool/export/home`, line 9, the available storage dropped to 143MB from 560MB with 107MB used. Compare line 5 with line 17 of the output to see the effect of setting the quota to 250MB. User layne's quota has not been affected since his quota is set at 20MB. Users ken and watanabe now have an upper limit of 143MB for available space.

4.1.2 The `reservation` and `refreservation` Settings

`reservation` and `refreservation` are two ZFS file system properties that control the minimum allocated storage blocks. The `reservation` property is the absolute minimum that a file system can consume, including descendents, snapshots, and clones. The `refreservation` property limits only the space consumed by the file system, not including descendents, snapshots, and clones. You can use these properties to guarantee a minimum amount of storage to a file system.

4.1.2.1 Using the `reservation` Setting

The most basic case is setting a reservation on a file system. This example sets a simple reservation on a file system:

```
 1   $ zfs list
 2   NAME                             USED   AVAIL   REFER   MOUNTPOINT
 3   homepool                         108M    560M   26.9K   /homepool
 4   homepool/export                  107M    560M   28.4K   /export
 5   homepool/export/home             107M    143M   50.9K   /export/home
 6   homepool/export/home/ken        8.17M    143M   8.17M   /export/home/ken
 7   homepool/export/home/layne      20.1M   1.82M   18.2M   /export/home/layne
 8   homepool/export/home/watanabe   78.8M    143M   71.2M   /export/home/watanabe
 ...Output deleted...
 9   $ pfexec zfs reservation=100m homepool/export/home/ken
10   $ zfs get reservation,refreservation homepool/export/home/ken
11   NAME                          PROPERTY          VALUE     SOURCE
12   homepool/export/home/ken      reservation       100M      local
13   homepool/export/home/ken      refreservation    none      default
14   watanabe@opensolaris:~$
15   watanabe@opensolaris:~$ zfs list
16   NAME                             USED   AVAIL   REFER   MOUNTPOINT
17   homepool                         200M    468M   26.9K   /homepool
18   homepool/export                  199M    468M   28.4K   /export
19   homepool/export/home             199M   51.1M   50.9K   /export/home
20   homepool/export/home/ken        8.17M    143M   8.17M   /export/home/ken
21   homepool/export/home/layne      20.1M   1.82M   18.2M   /export/home/layne
22   homepool/export/home/watanabe   78.8M   51.1M   71.2M   /export/home/watanabe
 ...Output deleted...
```

After setting the reservation for `homepool/export/home/ken` to 100MB, the 100MB was charged to the parent directory (`homepool/export/home/ken`) on line 26. On line 27, no change is made to the available storage for `homepool/export/home/ken`. On line 28, `homepool/export/home/layne`, available space is unchanged because of the quota set in the previous example. On line 29, `homepool/export/home/watanabe` has 51.1MB available. This space is calculated with the original available (line 8) for user watanabe minus (the reservation minus the used storage by ken):

$$143MB - (100MB - 8.17MB) = 51.17MB$$

4.1.2.2 Using the `refreservation` Setting

Using the `refreservation` setting limits the used storage in just the file system. The setting has no effect on any descendents, snapshots, or clones. The following example sets the `refreservation` property to 5MB.

First, clear out the previous `reservation` setting, and set `refreservation` to 50MB:

```
1    $ pfexec zfs reservation=none homepool/export/home/ken
2    $ zfs get reservation,refreservation homepool/export/home/ken
3    NAME                         PROPERTY          VALUE      SOURCE
4    homepool/export/home/ken     reservation       none       default
5    homepool/export/home/ken     refreservation    none       default
6    $ zfs list
7    NAME                          USED   AVAIL   REFER   MOUNTPOINT
8    homepool                      108M   560M    26.9K   /homepool
9    homepool/export               107M   560M    28.4K   /export
10   homepool/export/home          107M   143M    50.9K   /export/home
11   homepool/export/home/ken      8.17M  143M    8.17M   /export/home/ken
12   homepool/export/home/layne    20.1M  1.82M   18.2M   /export/home/layne
13   homepool/export/home/watanabe 78.8M  143M    71.2M   /export/home/watanabe
...Output deleted...
14   $ pfexec zfs refreservation=50m homepool/export/home/ken
15   $ zfs get reservation,refreservation homepool/export/home/ken
16   NAME                         PROPERTY          VALUE      SOURCE
17   homepool/export/home/ken     reservation       none       default
18   homepool/export/home/ken     refreservation    50M        local
19   $ zfs list
20   NAME                          USED   AVAIL   REFER   MOUNTPOINT
21   homepool                      150M   518M    26.9K   /homepool
22   homepool/export               149M   518M    28.4K   /export
23   homepool/export/home          149M   101M    50.9K   /export/home
24   homepool/export/home/ken      50M    143M    8.17M   /export/home/ken
25   homepool/export/home/layne    20.1M  1.82M   18.2M   /export/home/layne
26   homepool/export/home/watanabe 78.8M  101M    71.2M   /export/home/watanabe
...Output deleted...             844M   9.13G   16K     -
```

After setting the `refreservation` property to 50MB, on line 31, the used space charged to `homepool/export/home/ken` grows by 42MB to 50MB. The parent directory's used number grows by 42MB to 149MB from 107MB. The file system `homepool/export/home/layne` again stays the same on line 32. On line 33, the next file system, `homepool/export/home/watanabe`, has the available storage reduced by 42MB to 101MB.

4.2 Enabling Compression on a ZFS File System

You can reduce the amount of space that is consumed by a ZFS file system by using the compression feature. This property is disabled by default. When enabled, the default compression algorithm is `lzjb`. The `lzjb` algorithm strikes a balance between performance and compression. The best compression will consume more CPU cycles to achieve this and will affect the performance of the file system. Using a balanced compression algorithm like `lzjb`, file system performance might actually increase depending on the data. The other compression algorithm supported is `gzip`. This is the same algorithm as that used by the `gzip` command. You can specify the level of compression using the `gzip` algorithm from 1 (fastest) to 9 (best compression). By default, `gzip-6` is used when `gzip` is set.

Enabling compression helps manage available space for a file system. When compression is enabled on a file system, the space usage numbers will differ depending on the command used to calculate size.

The following example illustrates how to enable compression using the `lzjb` and `gzip-9` algorithms. The files in Table 4.1 were copied after enabling the `compression` property on the file system.

```
$ pfexec zfs compression=on homepool/export/home/judy
$ pfexec zfs compression=gzip-9 homepool/export/home/judy
```

Table 4.1 File Sizes and Disk Usage Comparisons

Filename	Orignal ls –lh	lzjb ls –lh	gzip-9 ls –lh	Original du -h	lzjb du -h	gzip-9 du -h
1.Millsap2000.01.03-RAID5.pdf	42KB	42KB	42KB	43KB	37KB	28KB
Anna_Karenina_T.pdf	4.4MB	4.4MB	4.4MB	4.4MB	4.0MB	2.7MB
Crime_and_Punishment_T.pdf	2.5MB	2.5MB	2.5MB	2.6MB	2.3MB	1.6MB
Emma_T.pdf	1.9MB	1.9MB	1.9MB	1.9MB	1.8MB	1.2MB
Moby_Dick_NT.pdf	2.3MB	2.3MB	2.3MB	2.3MB	2.1MB	1.4MB
Shakespeare William Romeo and Juliet.pdf	259KB	259KB	259KB	387KB	265KB	200KB
War_and_Peace_NT.pdf	6.3MB	6.3MB	6.3MB	6.3MB	5.8MB	4.0MB
zfs_last.pdf	3.1MB	3.1MB	3.1MB	3.2MB	3.1MB	2.9MB
zfs_lc_preso.pdf	2.3M	2.3M	2.3M	2.3M	2.3M	1.8M

The listing output is the same in all cases, but the disk usage is less with compression turned on. The best compression is `gzip-9`.

Another statistic you can use is the `compressratio` property status of the ZFS file system. This will show the compression efficiency of the data on the file system. Table 4.2 provides an idea of the kind of compression ratios available from `lzjb` and `gzip-9`.

```
$ zfs get compressratio zfs_filesystem
```

Table 4.2 Compression Ratio Output

Compression	Compression Ratio
Original (no compression)	1.00
`lzjb`	1.08
`gzip-9`	1.47

You need to be careful when moving or copying data from a compressed file system. The compression could cause backup or archive programs to underestimate the size of the media and the time that is needed to execute the job. Using the `compressratio` and disk usage will give an approximate size of the uncompressed data as it moved to an archive. Take the output of `du -s` of the file system or directory, and multiply by the compression ratio to get an approximation of the size of the data that needs to be copied.

4.3 Working with ZFS Snapshots

Users can manage their own deleted, destroyed, and modified data by implementing snapshots for home directories. A **snapshot** is a read-only copy of a ZFS file system and is created using the `zfs snapshot` command.

4.3.1 Managing the Snapshot Directory

Once a snapshot is taken, a `.zfs` directory is created in the root of the file system. This directory is hidden by default from most commands unless the `.zfs` directory is specifically named. It is best to keep the snapshot directory hidden so that archive programs, such as `tar`, `cpio`, and `gzip`, do not copy the same data multiple times.

For example, listing files in a home directory yields normal files:

```
cindy@opensolaris:~$ ls -a
.    .bash_history  Books  local.login   .profile
..   .bashrc    local.cshrc  local.profile
cindy@opensolaris:~$ ls .zfs
snapshot
```

In the example, specifying the `.zfs` directory with the `ls` command shows the snapshot directory.

You can make the `.zfs` directory visible by changing the `snapdir` property from `hidden` to `visible`:

```
$ zfs get snapdir homepool/export/home/cindy
NAME                             PROPERTY  VALUE    SOURCE
homepool/export/home/cindy       snapdir   hidden   local
$ pfexec zfs snapdir=visible homepool/export/home/cindy
$ zfs get snapdir homepool/export/home/cindy
NAME                             PROPERTY  VALUE    SOURCE
homepool/export/home/cindy       snapdir   visible  local
???
cindy@opensolaris:~$ ls -a
.     .bash_history  Books  local.login    .profile
..    .bashrc        local.cshrc  local.profile  .zfs
```

When the `snapdir` property is set to `visible`, the `ls` command displays the `.zfs` directory.

The following example is the output from a `tar` archive of a home directory with the snap directory hidden:

```
cindy@opensolaris:~$ tar cvf /var/tmp/cindy.hidden.tar .
./
./local.cshrc
././.profile
././.bashrc
./Books/
./Books/Anna_Karenina_T.pdf
./Books/zfs_lc_preso.pdf
./Books/Shakespeare William Romeo and Juliet.pdf
./Books/zfs_last.pdf
./Books/War_and_Peace_NT.pdf
./Books/1.Millsap2000.01.03-RAID5.pdf
./Books/Crime_and_Punishment_T.pdf
./Books/Moby_Dick_NT.pdf
./Books/Emma_T.pdf
././.bash_history
./local.login
./local.profile
```

The following example is the same `tar` command with the snap directory visible. The archive now copies the `.zfs` directory, doubling the size of the archive. This file system has only one snapshot. If the file system had additional snapshots, the archive size could grow larger.

```
cindy@opensolaris:~$ tar cvf /var/tmp/cindy.visible.tar .
./
././.zfs/
././.zfs/snapshot/
././.zfs/snapshot/sunday/
././.zfs/snapshot/sunday/local.cshrc
```

continues

```
./.zfs/snapshot/sunday/.profile
./.zfs/snapshot/sunday/.bashrc
./.zfs/snapshot/sunday/Books/
./.zfs/snapshot/sunday/Books/Anna_Karenina_T.pdf
./.zfs/snapshot/sunday/Books/zfs_lc_preso.pdf
./.zfs/snapshot/sunday/Books/Shakespeare William Romeo and Juliet.pdf
./.zfs/snapshot/sunday/Books/zfs_last.pdf
./.zfs/snapshot/sunday/Books/War_and_Peace_NT.pdf
./.zfs/snapshot/sunday/Books/1.Millsap2000.01.03-RAID5.pdf
./.zfs/snapshot/sunday/Books/Crime_and_Punishment_T.pdf
./.zfs/snapshot/sunday/Books/Moby_Dick_NT.pdf
./.zfs/snapshot/sunday/Books/Emma_T.pdf
./.zfs/snapshot/sunday/.bash_history
./.zfs/snapshot/sunday/local.login
./.zfs/snapshot/sunday/local.profile
./local.cshrc
./.profile
./.bashrc
./Books/
./Books/Anna_Karenina_T.pdf
./Books/zfs_lc_preso.pdf
./Books/Shakespeare William Romeo and Juliet.pdf
./Books/zfs_last.pdf
./Books/War_and_Peace_NT.pdf
./Books/1.Millsap2000.01.03-RAID5.pdf
./Books/Crime_and_Punishment_T.pdf
./Books/Moby_Dick_NT.pdf
./Books/Emma_T.pdf
./.bash_history
./local.login
./local.profile
cindy@opensolaris:~$


cindy@opensolaris:~$ ls -lFh /var/tmp/cindy*
-rw-r--r-- 1 cindy other 23M 2009-02-15 18:01 /var/tmp/cindy.hidden.tar
-rw-r--r-- 1 cindy other 46M 2009-02-15 18:01 /var/tmp/cindy.visible.tar
```

4.3.2 Recovering Files from Snapshots

Users can recover their own files from ZFS snapshots, which frees you from simple file recovery tasks. When file system snapshots are available, each user has their own snapshot directory. This means each of the users can securely recover their own files from a snapshot.

The snapshot files are read-only and cannot be modified in place. To be able to modify any file in the snapshot directory, the file needs to be copied to a regular directory that is not in the `.zfs` snapshot directory. Chapter 7 covers the administration and use of Time Slider a GUI-based tool that is designed to recover files from a snapshot.

You can use the ZFS `rollback` subcommand to recover whole environments from a snapshot.

4.3.2.1 Delegating ZFS Commands

By default a regular user does not have the capability to roll back a file system snapshot, so you, the administrator, can grant regular users the capability to roll back their own file system snapshots. For more information about delegating ZFS permissions to users, see the ZFS man page.

In the following example, user cindy is delegated the permissions to roll back her file system snapshot. The subcommands that are delegated are `mount`, `snapshot`, and `rollback` on the user's home directory.

```
$ pfexec zfs allow cindy mount,rollback,snapshot homepool/export/home/cindy
$ zfs allow homepool/export/home/cindy
-------------------------------------------------------------
Local+Descendent permissions on (homepool/export/home/cindy)
     user cindy mount,rollback,snapshot
-------------------------------------------------------------
```

4.3.2.2 Rolling Back a File System

In this example, you'll roll back a file system to its last known good snapshot by using the `rollback` subcommand that was just delegated to user cindy.

In this example, the entire home directory is removed accidentally:

```
cindy@opensolaris:~$ rm -rf *
cindy@opensolaris:~$ rm -rf .*
rm: cannot remove directory `.'
rm: cannot remove directory `..'
$ ls -Fa
./  ../
```

Now you, or the home directory owner, must find the most recent snapshot and select it for a rollback. You can do this with the `zfs list` command:

```
$ zfs list -t snapshot
NAME                                       USED  AVAIL  REFER  MOUNTPOINT
homepool/export/home/cindy@sunday          23.1M     -  23.1M  -
homepool/export/home/layne@samplesnap      1.91M     -  20.1M  -
homepool/export/home/watanabe@today        7.59M     -  31.6M  -
rpool@today                                  18K     -  75.5K  -
rpool/ROOT@today                               0     -    18K  -
rpool/ROOT/opensolaris@today                   0     -  2.67G  -
rpool/ROOT/opensolaris-1@install           72.3M     -  2.21G  -
rpool/ROOT/opensolaris-1@opensolaris1      12.1M     -  2.24G  -
rpool/ROOT/opensolaris-1@2009-01-30-13:24:22  100M   -  2.68G  -
rpool/ROOT/opensolaris-1@today             23.4M     -  2.74G  -
rpool/ROOT/opensolaris-1@today1            32.0M     -  2.79G  -
rpool/ROOT/opensolaris1@today              3.85M     -  2.68G  -
rpool/dump@today                             16K     -   844M  -
rpool/swap@today                               0     -    16K  -
cindy@opensolaris:~$ zfs rollback homepool/export/home/cindy@sunday
```

To identify the snapshots by date and time, use `zfs get creation` to retrieve the creation date and time of the snapshot:

```
$ zfs get creation homepool/export/home/cindy@sunday
NAME                                  PROPERTY  VALUE                SOURCE
homepool/export/home/cindy@sunday creation  Sun Feb 1 15:56 2009      -
```

Check the home directory for the restored files:

```
cindy@opensolaris:~$ ls -Fa
./    .bash_history  Books/       local.login     .profile
../   .bashrc        local.cshrc  local.profile
```

4.4 Sharing ZFS Home Directories

ZFS home directories are shared by using Network File System (NFS) services, as is done with Unix File System (UFS). You can set up the automounter so that the home directories appear the same on the server as they do on client systems. When users log in to the server, they can find the home directory using the same password entry used on the client. Using the `/home` directory to mount user directories, the automounter maps `server:/export/home/user_name` to `/home/user_name`. In this example, only files are used.

1. Edit the `/etc/passwd` file on the server to change all the user home directories from `/export/home/user_name` to `/home/user_name`. For more information on the passwd file, use `man -s 4 passwd`. Distribute the new password file to the other client systems.

```
watanabe:x:101:10:scott watanabe:/home/watanabe:/bin/bash
layne:x:65535:1:Layne :/home/layne:/bin/bash
judy:x:65536:1:Judy:/home/judy:/bin/bash
cindy:x:65537:1:Cindy:/home/cindy:/bin/bash
ken:x:65538:1:Ken:/home/ken:/bin/bash
```

2. Edit `/etc/auto_home`, and add the following line:
   `opensolaris:/home/&`

   The server name in this example is *opensolaris*:

```
# Home directory map for automounter
#
*       opensolaris:/export/home/&
+auto_home
```

The star (*) is a wildcard key, and the ampersand (&) takes the key (`user_name`) and makes a replacement. Copy this file to the other clients.

3. Set the `sharenfs` property to each home directory file system:

```
# zfs sharenfs=on homepool/export/home/cindy
# zfs sharenfs=on homepool/export/home/judy
# zfs sharenfs=on homepool/export/home/layne
# zfs sharenfs=on homepool/export/home/ken
# zfs sharenfs=on homepool/export/home/watanabe
```

4. Reboot the server to start the automounter.

    Log in as a user to test the configuration.

4.5 References

Here are some references for more information:

- **ZFS Administration Guide:**
  `http://docs.sun.com/app/docs/doc/819-5461`
- **ZFS Best Practices Wiki:**
  `www.solarisinternals.com/wiki/index.php/ZFS_Best_Practices_Guide`

Exploring Zpool
Advanced Concepts

In this chapter, you will explore techniques for creating the best possible pool configurations. The examples shown in this chapter are from the ZFS Configuration Guide at `www.solarisinternals.com/wiki/index.php/ZFS_Configuration_Guide`. *I will walk you through the commands that create the configuration and explain why it works.*

There are many ways to configure ZFS pools, some better than others, but it is my hope that from this chapter you will get a better idea for setting up a ZFS pool that suits your needs.

5.1 X4500 RAID-Z2 Configuration Example

This example uses a Sun x4500 that is fully populated with 250GB disks. The x4500 is an x64 system with two dual-core AMD Opteron processors: Model 290 at 2.8GHz with 48 hot-pluggable SATA II disks. The single point of failure for the storage is the motherboard. The disks' pool is spread over all the controllers, except for the system disks. This configuration is not designed for speed but for maximum disk availability with comfortable redundancy. The example creates a single mirror for the boot/system disk and ZFS pool with seven RAID-Z2 vdevs and four disk spares.

Six SATA II controllers are capable of handling eight disks per controller. Each disk has its own line into the controller (see Figure 5.1). If a cable goes bad, only a single disk is affected by the defect.

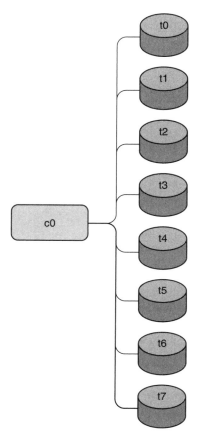

Figure 5.1 SATA controller with eight disks

In Figure 5.2, the drawing is altered to line up the disks with the controller inline. There are six controllers: c0, c1, c4, c5, c6, and c7. Each controller has eight target disks, starting from t0 to t7. The configuration has 48 disks total.

The boot disks are described as Solaris Volume Manager (SVM) mirrored. This now can easily be ZFS boot disks today in Solaris 10. Disks c4t0d0 and c5t0d0 are mirrored as the boot/system disks in Figure 5.3.

The first `zpool` command will create the new pool called *rpool* and create four RAIDZ2 vdevs:

```
# zpool create rpool \
raidz2 c0t1d0 c1t1d0 c4t1d0 c5t1d0 c6t1d0 c7t1d0 \
raidz2 c0t2d0 c1t2d0 c4t2d0 c5t2d0 c6t2d0 c7t2d0 \
raidz2 c0t3d0 c1t3d0 c4t3d0 c5t3d0 c6t3d0 c7t3d0 \
raidz2 c0t4d0 c1t4d0 c4t4d0 c5t4d0 c6t4d0 c7t4d0
```

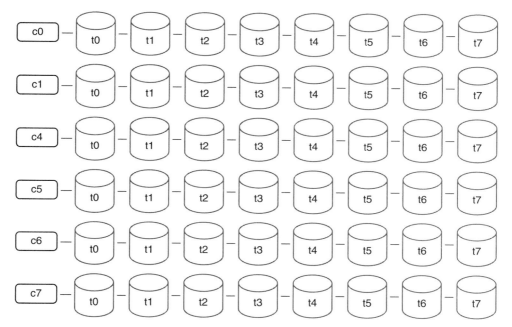

Figure 5.2 X4500 disk controllers and eight target disks per controller

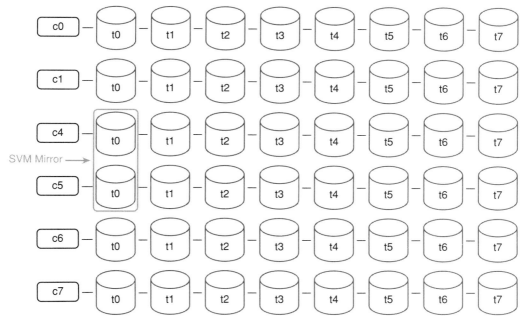

Figure 5.3 The boot disks c4t0d0 and c5t0d0 are circled as a mirror created by SVM

The command line has been parsed to see the vdev creation for the ZFS pool. Notice the four `raidz2` subcommands with six disks per vdev. Each `raidz2` sub-command uses disk targets in the same column (see Figure 5.4).

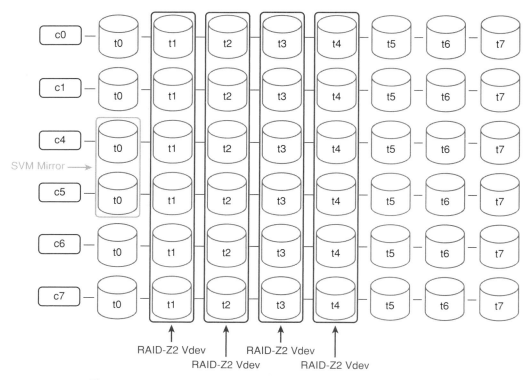

Figure 5.4 Creation of a ZFS pool with four RAID-Z2 vdevs

The first vdev uses all the disk targets (starting with t1). Each of the next vdevs spans the next three target numbers: 2, 3, and 4.

```
1    # zpool status
2    pool: rpool
3    state: ONLINE
4    scrub: none requested
5    config:
6
7    NAME          STATE      READ WRITE CKSUM
8    rpool         ONLINE        0     0     0
9      raidz2      ONLINE        0     0     0
10       c0t1d0    ONLINE        0     0     0
```

continues

```
11        c1t1d0    ONLINE      0    0    0
12        c4t1d0    ONLINE      0    0    0
13        c5t1d0    ONLINE      0    0    0
14        c6t1d0    ONLINE      0    0    0
15        c7t1d0    ONLINE      0    0    0
16   raidz2        ONLINE      0    0    0
17        c0t2d0    ONLINE      0    0    0
18        c1t2d0    ONLINE      0    0    0
19        c4t2d0    ONLINE      0    0    0
20        c5t2d0    ONLINE      0    0    0
21        c6t2d0    ONLINE      0    0    0
22        c7t2d0    ONLINE      0    0    0
23   raidz2        ONLINE      0    0    0
24        c0t3d0    ONLINE      0    0    0
25        c1t3d0    ONLINE      0    0    0
26        c4t3d0    ONLINE      0    0    0
27        c5t3d0    ONLINE      0    0    0
28        c6t3d0    ONLINE      0    0    0
29        c7t3d0    ONLINE      0    0    0
30   raidz2        ONLINE      0    0    0
31        c0t4d0    ONLINE      0    0    0
32        c1t4d0    ONLINE      0    0    0
33        c4t4d0    ONLINE      0    0    0
34        c5t4d0    ONLINE      0    0    0
35        c6t4d0    ONLINE      0    0    0
36        c7t4d0    ONLINE      0    0    0
37
38 errors: No known data errors
```

In the output of `zpool status`, on lines 9, 16, 23, and 30, the RAID-Z2 vdevs correspond to the RAID-Z2 vdevs in Figure 5.4. Each of the vdev disks has the same target number and different controller numbers. In this ZFS pool, each of the vdev disks can be damaged before any data is lost. Also, if a controller is damaged, the pool can still function.

In the next four `zpool` commands, you add three more RAID-Z2 vdevs across all six controllers and four disks to the spare pools:

```
1   # zpool add rpool raidz2 c0t5d0 c1t5d0 c4t5d0 c5t5d0 c6t5d0 c7t5d0
2   # zpool add rpool raidz2 c0t6d0 c1t6d0 c4t6d0 c5t6d0 c6t6d0 c7t6d0
3   # zpool add rpool raidz2 c0t7d0 c1t7d0 c4t7d0 c5t7d0 c6t7d0 c7t7d0
4   # zpool add rpool spare c0t0d0 c1t0d0 c6t0d0 c7t0d0
```

In the following figures, the ZFS pool configuration is shown after each command line is executed.

In Figure 5.5, a new RAID-Z2 vdev is added to the ZFS pool rpool after executing line 1. All the disks in this vdev are the target 5 (t5) disks across all six SATA controllers.

In Figure 5.6, a new RAID-Z2 vdev is added to ZFS pool rpool after executing line 2. All the disks in this vdev are the target 6 (t6) disks across all six SATA controllers.

In Figure 5.7, a new RAID-Z2 vdev is added to ZFS pool rpool after executing line 3. All the disks in this vdev are the target 6 (t6) disks across all six SATA controllers.

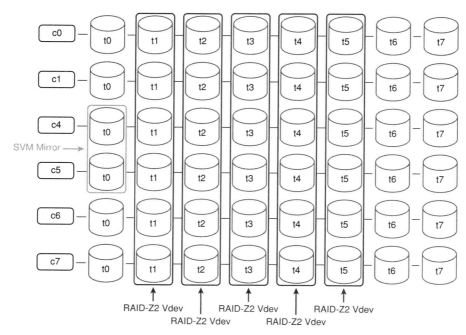

Figure 5.5 After executing line 1, a RAID-Z2 vdev using the target 5 (t5) disks is added to the ZFS pool

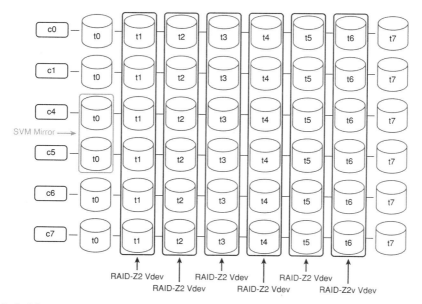

Figure 5.6 After executing line 2, a RAID-Z2 vdev using the target 6 (t6) disks is added to the ZFS pool

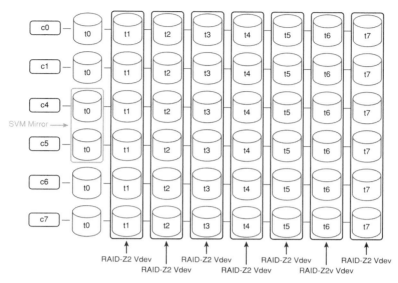

Figure 5.7 After executing line 3, a RAID-Z2 vdev using the target 7 (t7) disks is added to the ZFS pool

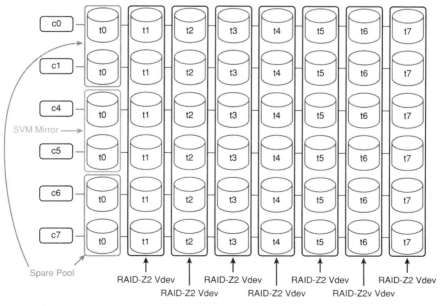

Figure 5.8 After executing line 4, four spares are added to the ZFS pool

After executing lines 1, 2, and 3, the ZFS pool is almost complete. Next, executing line 4 will add four spare disks to the pool rpool. Figure 5.8 shows the configuration after the spares are added.

Running a `status` command on the ZFS pool, you can now see the completed rpool. The four spares are listed starting at line 48.

```
 1    # zpool status
 2    pool: rpool
 3    state: ONLINE
 4    scrub: none requested
 5    config:
 6
 7    NAME                STATE     READ WRITE CKSUM
 8    rpool               ONLINE       0     0     0
 9       raidz2           ONLINE       0     0     0
10          c0t1d0        ONLINE       0     0     0
11          c1t1d0        ONLINE       0     0     0
12          c4t1d0        ONLINE       0     0     0
13          c5t1d0        ONLINE       0     0     0
14          c6t1d0        ONLINE       0     0     0
15          c7t1d0        ONLINE       0     0     0
16       raidz2           ONLINE       0     0     0
17          c0t2d0        ONLINE       0     0     0
18          c1t2d0        ONLINE       0     0     0
19          c4t2d0        ONLINE       0     0     0
20          c5t2d0        ONLINE       0     0     0
21          c6t2d0        ONLINE       0     0     0
22          c7t2d0        ONLINE       0     0     0
23       raidz2           ONLINE       0     0     0
24          c0t3d0        ONLINE       0     0     0
25          c1t3d0        ONLINE       0     0     0
26          c4t3d0        ONLINE       0     0     0
27          c5t3d0        ONLINE       0     0     0
28          c6t3d0        ONLINE       0     0     0
29          c7t3d0        ONLINE       0     0     0
30       raidz2           ONLINE       0     0     0
31          c0t4d0        ONLINE       0     0     0
32          c1t4d0        ONLINE       0     0     0
33          c4t4d0        ONLINE       0     0     0
34          c5t4d0        ONLINE       0     0     0
35          c6t4d0        ONLINE       0     0     0
36          c7t4d0        ONLINE       0     0     0
37       raidz2           ONLINE       0     0     0
38          c0t5d0        ONLINE       0     0     0
39          c1t5d0        ONLINE       0     0     0
40          c4t5d0        ONLINE       0     0     0
41          c5t5d0        ONLINE       0     0     0
42          c6t5d0        ONLINE       0     0     0
43          c7t5d0        ONLINE       0     0     0
44       raidz2           ONLINE       0     0     0
45          c0t6d0        ONLINE       0     0     0
46          c1t6d0        ONLINE       0     0     0
47          c4t6d0        ONLINE       0     0     0
48          c5t6d0        ONLINE       0     0     0
49          c6t6d0        ONLINE       0     0     0
50          c7t6d0        ONLINE       0     0     0
51       raidz2           ONLINE       0     0     0
52          c0t7d0        ONLINE       0     0     0
53          c1t7d0        ONLINE       0     0     0
```

continues

```
54        c4t7d0     ONLINE      0     0     0
55        c5t7d0     ONLINE      0     0     0
56        c6t7d0     ONLINE      0     0     0
57        c7t7d0     ONLINE      0     0     0
58      spares
59        c0t0d0     AVAIL
60        c1t0d0     AVAIL
61        c6t0d0     AVAIL
62        c7t0d0     AVAIL
63
64   errors: No known data errors
```

Creating the RAID-Z2 vdevs across the target disks columns also has an advantage of spreading the I/O across all the SATA controllers and not causing a single controller to be a bottleneck.

5.2 X4500 Mirror Configuration Example

Again, in this example, the single point of failure for the storage is the motherboard. The disks' pool is spread over multiple controllers. This configuration is designed for speed and maximum redundancy. Also, the data I/O will be spread across all six controllers for maximum performance. The example creates a single mirror for the boot/system disk and ZFS pool with 14 three-way mirrored vdevs and 4 disk spares.

This example starts with mirrored disks created by Solaris Volume Manager in Figure 5.9 as in the previous example.

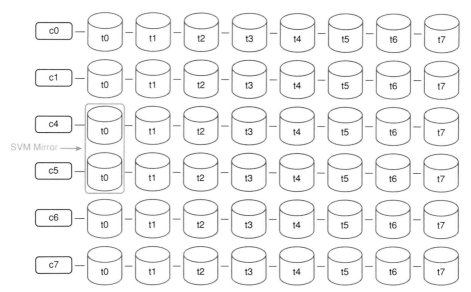

Figure 5.9 The boot disks c4t0d0 and c5t0d0 are circled as a mirror created by SVM

Next you create a ZFS pool named *mpool* with seven three-way mirrors using the following command:

```
# zpool create mpool \
mirror c0t1d0 c1t1d0 c4t1d0 \
mirror c0t2d0 c1t2d0 c4t2d0 \
mirror c0t3d0 c1t3d0 c4t3d0 \
mirror c0t4d0 c1t4d0 c4t4d0 \
mirror c0t5d0 c1t5d0 c4t5d0 \
mirror c0t6d0 c1t6d0 c4t6d0 \
mirror c0t7d0 c1t7d0 c4t7d0
```

The command line was formatted to make each three-way mirrored vdev clear. The `zpool status` command shows the newly created ZFS pool mpool with the seven vdevs:

```
# zpool status
  pool: mpool
 state: ONLINE
 scrub: none requested
config:

        NAME         STATE     READ WRITE CKSUM
        mpool        ONLINE       0     0     0
          mirror     ONLINE       0     0     0
            c0t1d0   ONLINE       0     0     0
            c1t1d0   ONLINE       0     0     0
            c4t1d0   ONLINE       0     0     0
          mirror     ONLINE       0     0     0
            c0t2d0   ONLINE       0     0     0
            c1t2d0   ONLINE       0     0     0
            c4t2d0   ONLINE       0     0     0
          mirror     ONLINE       0     0     0
            c0t3d0   ONLINE       0     0     0
            c1t3d0   ONLINE       0     0     0
            c4t3d0   ONLINE       0     0     0
          mirror     ONLINE       0     0     0
            c0t4d0   ONLINE       0     0     0
            c1t4d0   ONLINE       0     0     0
            c4t4d0   ONLINE       0     0     0
          mirror     ONLINE       0     0     0
            c0t5d0   ONLINE       0     0     0
            c1t5d0   ONLINE       0     0     0
            c4t5d0   ONLINE       0     0     0
          mirror     ONLINE       0     0     0
            c0t6d0   ONLINE       0     0     0
            c1t6d0   ONLINE       0     0     0
            c4t6d0   ONLINE       0     0     0
          mirror     ONLINE       0     0     0
            c0t7d0   ONLINE       0     0     0
            c1t7d0   ONLINE       0     0     0
            c4t7d0   ONLINE       0     0     0

errors: No known data errors
```

Notice the indentation in the output. ZFS pool mpool has seven mirror vdevs, and each vdev has three disks. Figure 5.10 shows the vdevs in the diagram of the X4500.

In Figure 5.10, it is easy to see each mirrored vdev using three different SATA II controllers. A mirrored vdev could lose a maximum of two disks or a controller without losing any data in the ZFS pool.

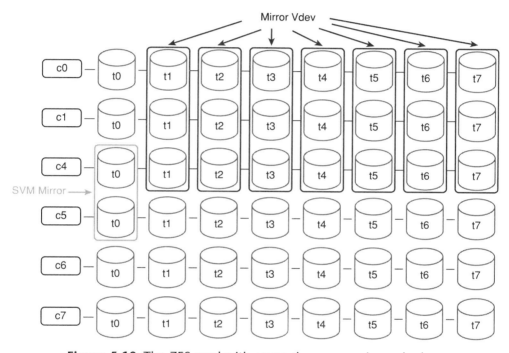

Figure 5.10 The ZFS pool with seven three-way mirrored vdevs

The next eight commands fill out the rest of the configuration of the X4500 with another seven three-way mirrored vdevs and four disks in a spare pool:

```
# zpool add mpool mirror c5t1d0 c6t1d0 c7t1d0
# zpool add mpool mirror c5t2d0 c6t2d0 c7t2d0
# zpool add mpool mirror c5t3d0 c6t3d0 c7t3d0
# zpool add mpool mirror c5t4d0 c6t4d0 c7t4d0
# zpool add mpool mirror c5t5d0 c6t5d0 c7t5d0
# zpool add mpool mirror c5t6d0 c6t6d0 c7t6d0
# zpool add mpool mirror c5t7d0 c6t7d0 c7t7d0
# zpool add mpool spare c0t0d0 c1t0d0 c6t0d0 c7t0d0
```

The `zpool status` command shows the ZFS pool mpool now with seven additional mirrored vdevs and a spare pool with four disks:

```
# zpool status
  pool: mpool
 state: ONLINE
 scrub: none requested
      config:

        NAME            STATE     READ WRITE CKSUM
        mpool           ONLINE       0     0     0
          mirror        ONLINE       0     0     0
            c0t1d0      ONLINE       0     0     0
            c1t1d0      ONLINE       0     0     0
            c4t1d0      ONLINE       0     0     0
          mirror        ONLINE       0     0     0
            c0t2d0      ONLINE       0     0     0
            c1t2d0      ONLINE       0     0     0
            c4t2d0      ONLINE       0     0     0
          mirror        ONLINE       0     0     0
            c0t3d0      ONLINE       0     0     0
            c1t3d0      ONLINE       0     0     0
            c4t3d0      ONLINE       0     0     0
          mirror        ONLINE       0     0     0
            c0t4d0      ONLINE       0     0     0
            c1t4d0      ONLINE       0     0     0
            c4t4d0      ONLINE       0     0     0
          mirror        ONLINE       0     0     0
            c0t5d0      ONLINE       0     0     0
            c1t5d0      ONLINE       0     0     0
            c4t5d0      ONLINE       0     0     0
          mirror        ONLINE       0     0     0
            c0t6d0      ONLINE       0     0     0
            c1t6d0      ONLINE       0     0     0
            c4t6d0      ONLINE       0     0     0
          mirror        ONLINE       0     0     0
            c0t7d0      ONLINE       0     0     0
            c1t7d0      ONLINE       0     0     0
            c4t7d0      ONLINE       0     0     0
          mirror        ONLINE       0     0     0
            c5t1d0      ONLINE       0     0     0
            c6t1d0      ONLINE       0     0     0
            c7t1d0      ONLINE       0     0     0
          mirror        ONLINE       0     0     0
            c5t2d0      ONLINE       0     0     0
            c6t2d0      ONLINE       0     0     0
            c7t2d0      ONLINE       0     0     0
          mirror        ONLINE       0     0     0
            c5t3d0      ONLINE       0     0     0
            c6t3d0      ONLINE       0     0     0
            c7t3d0      ONLINE       0     0     0
          mirror        ONLINE       0     0     0
            c5t4d0      ONLINE       0     0     0
            c6t4d0      ONLINE       0     0     0
            c7t4d0      ONLINE       0     0     0
          mirror        ONLINE       0     0     0
            c5t5d0      ONLINE       0     0     0
            c6t5d0      ONLINE       0     0     0
            c7t5d0      ONLINE       0     0     0
```

continues

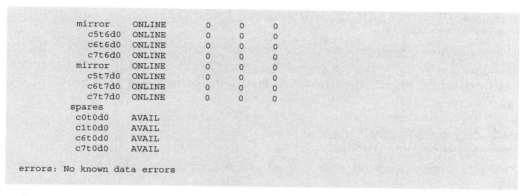

```
        mirror    ONLINE      0     0     0
          c5t6d0  ONLINE      0     0     0
          c6t6d0  ONLINE      0     0     0
          c7t6d0  ONLINE      0     0     0
        mirror    ONLINE      0     0     0
          c5t7d0  ONLINE      0     0     0
          c6t7d0  ONLINE      0     0     0
          c7t7d0  ONLINE      0     0     0
        spares
          c0t0d0          AVAIL
          c1t0d0          AVAIL
          c6t0d0          AVAIL
          c7t0d0          AVAIL

errors: No known data errors
```

Figure 5.11 shows the X4500 configuration completed.

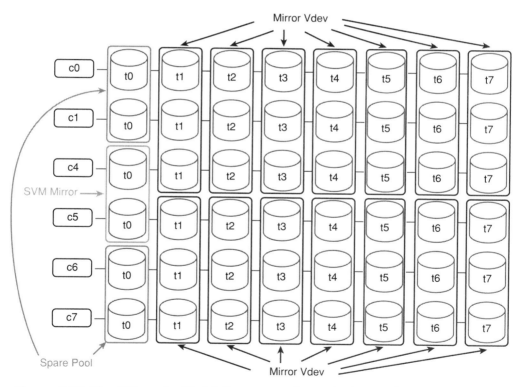

Figure 5.11 The ZFS pool with 14 three-way mirrored vdevs and a spare pool with 4 disks

5.3 X4500 Boot Mirror Alternative Example

Using a ZFS boot disk, you can create a normal two-way ZFS mirror and share the spare pool with the data ZFS pool of the previous two examples. In this way, you can increase the reliability of the whole system including the system disks.

5.4 ZFS and Array Storage

ZFS also works well with your current storage arrays. Any logical unit number (LUN) presented to ZFS is used like any other disk. These are some considerations when using storage arrays with ZFS:

- ZFS is not a shared file system. The LUNs presented are exclusive to the ZFS host.
- ZFS is oblivious to disk failures if hardware RAID is used. The LUN presented will look normal to ZFS, and any disk replacement will be handled at the array level. The array is responsible for rebuilding the LUN.
- A striped LUN is just a bigger disk. A disk failure in a striped LUN will be a failure of the whole LUN. The failed disk needs to be replaced and the LUN rebuilt before ZFS resilvering can take place.
- ZFS still needs its own redundancy. Even if the LUN is redundant (mirror or RAID-5), ZFS still needs to be configured in a mirror or a RAID-Z for best results.
- ZFS is MPxIO safe. In Solaris 10, MPxIO is integrated in the operating system. MPxIO provides a multipathing solution for storage devices accessible through multiple physical paths. See www.sun.com/bigadmin/xperts/ sessions/23_fibre/#7.

Another obvious disadvantage to using a hardware redundant configuration in ZFS is the available disk space. At each level of redundancy, available storage is decreased. When a hardware mirror is used with a ZFS mirror, the available space is 25 percent of the raw capacity.

6

Managing Solaris CIFS Server and Client

OpenSolaris has a built-in native CIFS client and server. The client is installed by default, and the server packages can be installed after interactive installation. OpenSolaris can manage CIFS by the command line or a GUI via the GNOME file manager. There is no anonymous user in the built-in server. If an anonymous user is required, then SAMBA would be the better option to configure.

The CIFS client and server are not available in Solaris 10.

6.1 Installing the CIFS Server Packages

OpenSolaris uses Image Packaging System (IPS). This is the next generation of package management for Solaris. You need two packages in order to install the SMB server: SUNWsmbs and SUNWsmbskr. The latter is a kernel package and will require a reboot before the server can be activated.

6.1.1 Installing the Server Packages with Package Manager

To install server packages with Package Manager, follow these steps:

1. To start Package Manager, select System > Administration > Package Manager. In the Search box, type smb (see Figure 6.1).
2. Select SUNWsmbs and SUNWsmbskr.

3. Click the Install/Update button. Package Manager will contact the repository at OpenSolaris.org and retrieve the packages' information (see Figure 6.2).

4. Click the Next button. Then wait for the packages to install.

5. Reboot the system.

6. Select System > Shutdown.

7. Click the Restart button to activate SMB in the kernel.

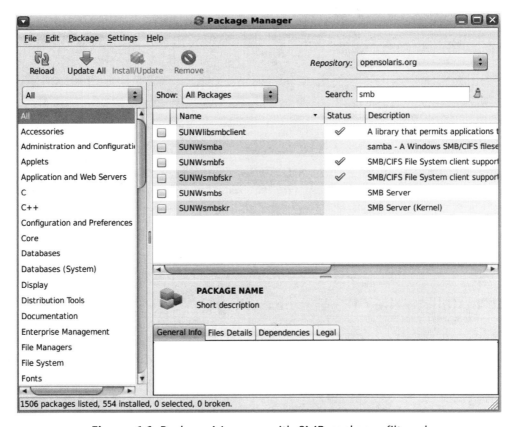

Figure 6.1 Package Manager with SMB packages filtered

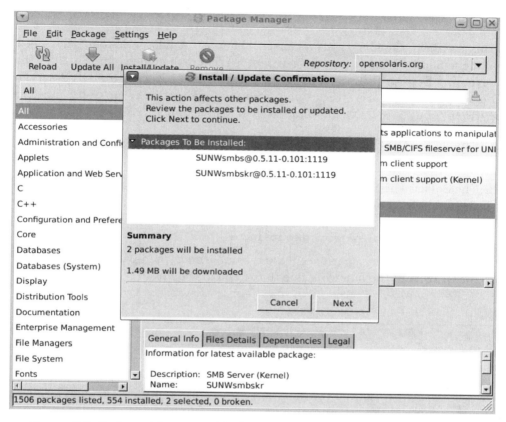

Figure 6.2 Package Manager with the server packages ready to be installed

6.1.2 Installing the Server Packages from the Command Line

Use the `pkg` command to retrieve and install packages from the OpenSolaris.org repository:

```
1   watanabe@opensolaris:~$ pfexec pkg install SUNWsmbs SUNWsmbskr
2   DOWNLOAD                                   PKGS     FILES    XFER (MB)
3   Completed                                  2/2      34/34    1.49/1.49
4
5   PHASE                                      ACTIONS
6   Install Phase                              80/80
7   PHASE                                      ITEMS
8   Reading Existing Index                     9/9
9   Indexing Packages                          2/2
```

Now reboot the system to activate the SMB server in the kernel.

6.2 Configuring the SMB Server in Workgroup Mode

In this scenario, the clients are primarily laptops (Windows or Mac) that need to mount the home directories with their laptops. There is no need for Windows Internet Naming Service (WINS) or Active Directory (AD). To create a CIFS server in AD mode, see the Solaris CIFS Administration Guide at `http://docs.sun.com/app/docs/doc/820-2429` for detailed task instruction.

1. Enable the CIFS service:

   # **svcadm enable -r smb/server**

2. The Solaris CIFS SMB service uses WORKGROUP as the default group. If the workgroup needs to be changed, use the following command to change the workgroup name:

   # **smbadm join -w workgroup-name**

3. Next edit the `/etc/pam.conf` file to enable encrypted passwords to be used for CIFS. Add the following line to the end of the file:

   ```
   other password required pam_smb_passwd.so.1      nowarn
   ```

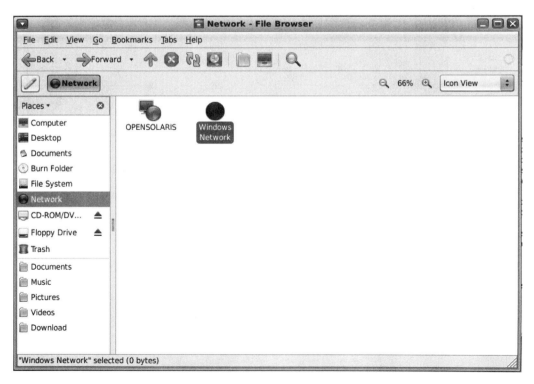

Figure 6.3 GNOME file manager with network and server OPENSOLARIS

4. Each user currently in the `/etc/passwd` file needs to reencrypt to be able to use the CIFS service:

   $ **pfexec passwd user-name**

   In Figure 6.3, you can see that the server OPENSOLARIS is an SMB server.

5. Select the server OPENSOLARIS to find any SMB shares that the server has.

   In Figure 6.4, no SMB shares are currently available to mount from OPEN-SOLARIS.

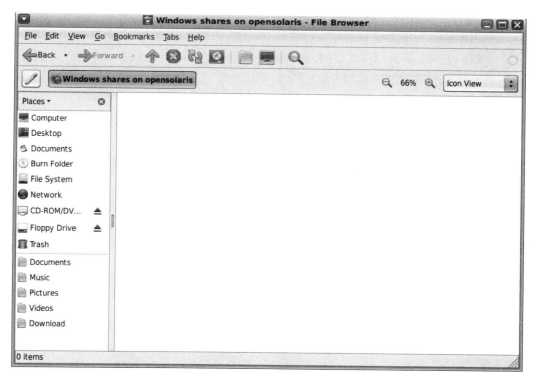

Figure 6.4 Selected OPENSOLARIS and with no available SMB shares

6.3 Sharing Home Directories

Sharing home directories using the OpenSolaris SMB server has been designed for ease of administration. The system creates a share when a user logs in and removes it when the user logs out.

1. To share all home directories, create and edit the `/etc/smbautohome` file. In the example OpenSolaris installation, all home directories are in `/export/home/username` file systems.

2. Edit `/etc/smbautohome`, and add the following line:

   `* /export/home/&`

   The star (`*`) and the ampersand (`&`) compose a shortcut to match a username with its home directory. Otherwise, each user would need their own entry in the `/etc/smbautohome` file.

3. Test the new home directory using the GNOME file manager. On the Go To line, type **smb://hostname/username**, which is `smb://opensolaris/judy` in the following example.

   After entering the SMB URL in the Go To box, you are presented with a login window, as illustrated in Figure 6.5.

4. Log in. In Figure 6.6, user judy is logging in to the workgroup domain WORKGROUP.

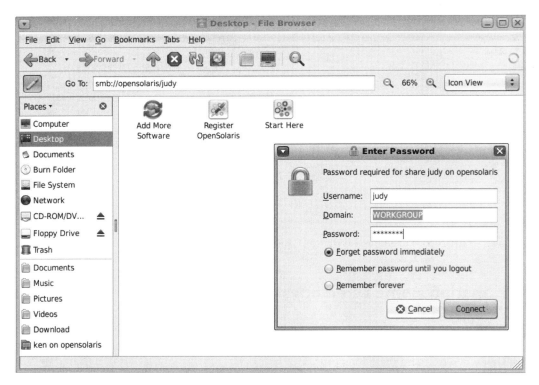

Figure 6.5 The GNOME file manager logging into an OpenSolaris SMB server

Figure 6.6 Login window for user judy

As shown in Figure 6.7, user judy is presented with her home directory. She can see only her own directory and cannot browse other users' directories. This makes for a cleaner interface for a user.

Figure 6.7 The file manager after user judy logs in

Another way to activate SMB shares is by setting the `sharesmb` property to `on`, using the `zfs set` command:

```
$ pfexec zfs set sharesmb=on homepool/export/home
$ pfexec zfs set sharesmb=on homepool/export/home/cindy
$ pfexec zfs set sharesmb=on homepool/export/home/judy
$ pfexec zfs set sharesmb=on homepool/export/home/ken
$ pfexec zfs set sharesmb=on homepool/export/home/layne
$ pfexec zfs set sharesmb=on homepool/export/home/watanabe
```

Figure 6.8 shows what the file manager will see if all the ZFS file systems are shared using the `sharesmb` setting.

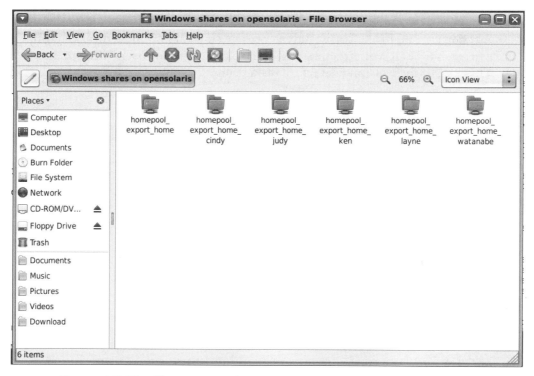

Figure 6.8 The file manager showing individual home directory shares

In Figure 6.8, the names listed are the ZFS file systems and may confuse some users. You should share common directories via the `smbshare` property.

Using Time Slider

Time Slider is a tool that users can use to retrieve deleted, damaged, or previous versions of a file or directory. Time Slider has two parts: a front-end GUI in the Nautilus file manager and a back end managed by Service Management Facility (SMF). Time Slider is currently available on OpenSolaris.

7.1 Enabling Time Slider Snapshots

You can enable and configure Time Slider snapshots using the Time Slider Setup GUI. In this chapter, I will show how to configure Time Slider only for home directories. The default configuration takes snapshots of all ZFS file systems.

The Time Slider schedule has five periodic snapshots (see Table 7.1). Each period has a different number of snapshots kept.

Table 7.1 Snapshot Types, Periodic Frequency, and Number Kept

Type of Snapshot	Frequency	Kept
Frequent	15 minutes	4
Hourly	60 minutes	24
Daily	Daily	31
Weekly	Weekly (1, 8, 15, 22, 29)	4
Monthly	Monthly (on the 1st)	12

To enable Time Slider snapshots, follow these steps:

1. Start the Time Slider Setup GUI as the administrative user of the system. From the GNOME desktop, select System > Administration > Time Slider Setup from the top menu bar (see Figure 7.1).

Figure 7.1 Starting the Time Slider Setup GUI

2. Next, select the Enable Time Slider check box, as shown in Figure 7.2, and click OK.

Figure 7.2 Enabling the Time Slider box

3. Click the Advanced Options button. Here you'll use Time Slider on home
    directories, so deselect everything but user home directories (see Figure 7.3).
    Then click the OK button.

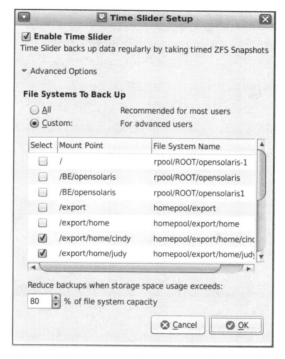

Figure 7.3 Advanced options in Time Slider

7.2 Enabling Nautilus Time Slider

By using the Nautilus file manager and the Time Slider plug-in, a user can recover
files from previous snapshots of the user's home directory. The recovered file or
directory will be placed on the user's desktop.

1. Start the Nautilus file manager, and set the mode to List View. From the
    Nautilus file manager menu, select View > List to set the List View mode.
    The List View mode will display information about the file or directory when
    the Time Slider box is selected.

    Figure 7.4 shows the Nautilus file manager in the List View mode.

2. Click the Time Slider icon. As shown in Figure 7.5, with the Time Slider icon
    selected, the slider appears.

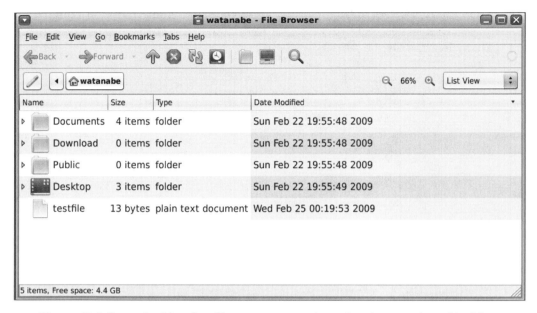

Figure 7.4 Start the Nautilus file manager, and set the view mode to List View

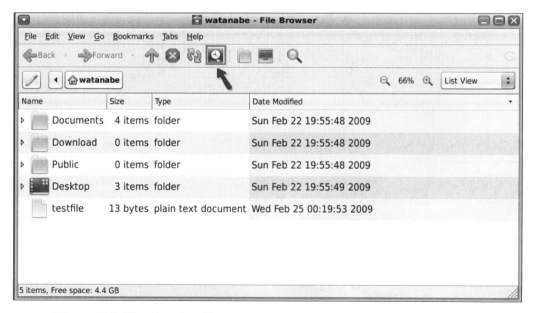

Figure 7.5 The Nautilus file manager with the Time Slider icon selected

3. In the "Restore information" column only, the file `testfile` has different versions available for restoration. Drag the slider to the desired time frame. When the slider is dragged to an older snapshot, a difference is noted from the latest version of the file or directory. For example, in Figure 7.6, the file `testfile` is compared with the current version of the file. The date timestamp and size differences are noted in the "Restore information" column.

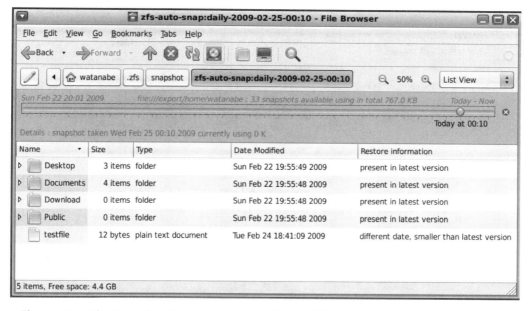

Figure 7.6 The Nautilus file manager with Time Slider and the slider moved to the desired time frame

4. Select the file `testfile` for restore. Then select Edit > Restore to Desktop, as shown in Figure 7.7.

5. In Figure 7.8, you see the file `testfile` restored to the desktop. It appears right below the Start Here icon.

7.3 Modifying the Snapshot Schedule

You can modify the ZFS snapshot schedule using SMF. You can gain finer control over the behavior of the autosnapshots by using the command line of SMF.

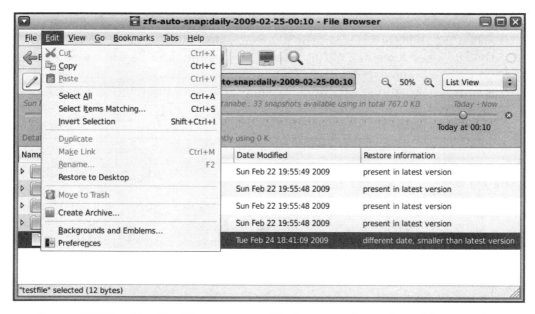

Figure 7.7 The Nautilus file manager with file `testfile` selected for restoring to the desktop

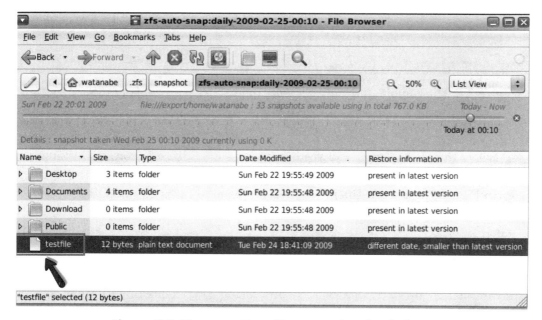

Figure 7.8 The `testfile` file restored to the desktop

7.3.1 Snapshot Basics

Check to see whether all default snapshot services are running. There should be five instances running by default for each of the five periodic snaps listed in Table 7.1.

```
$ svcs | grep snapshot
online         16:01:38 svc:/system/filesystem/zfs/auto-snapshot:monthly
online         16:01:39 svc:/system/filesystem/zfs/auto-snapshot:daily
online         16:01:41 svc:/system/filesystem/zfs/auto-snapshot:weekly
online         16:01:41 svc:/system/filesystem/zfs/auto-snapshot:hourly
online         16:01:43 svc:/system/filesystem/zfs/auto-snapshot:frequent
```

Each snapshot is executed from `cron` as user zfssnap. To check the `cron` schedule, use the `crontab` command. Do not edit the `crontab` for zfssnap. Each SMF instance manages the `cron` schedule. See the man page on `crontab` for more information on the entry format.

```
$ pfexec crontab -l zfssnap
0 0 1 1,2,3,4,5,6,7,8,9,10,11,12 * /lib/svc/method/zfs-auto-snapshot \
 svc:/system/filesystem/zfs/auto-snapshot:monthly
0 0 1,2,3,4,5,6,7,8,9,10,11,12,13,14, \
15,16,17,18,19,20,21,22,23,24,25,26,27,28,29,30,31 * * \
/lib/svc/method/zfs-auto-snapshot \
svc:/system/filesystem/zfs/auto-snapshot:daily
0 0 1,8,15,22,29 * * /lib/svc/method/zfs-auto-snapshot \
svc:/system/filesystem/zfs/auto-snapshot:weekly
0 0,1,2,3,4,5,6,7,8,9,10,11,12,13,14,15, \
16,17,18,19,20,21,22,23 * * * /lib/svc/method/zfs-auto-snapshot \
svc:/system/filesystem/zfs/auto-snapshot:hourly
0,15,30,45 * * * * /lib/svc/method/zfs-auto-snapshot \
svc:/system/filesystem/zfs/auto-snapshot:frequent
```

7.3.2 Changing the Period

Change the period for the frequent snapshots service to every ten minutes. Use the `svccfg` command to change the service properties. First, you list the properties for the frequent method by using the `svccfg` command, as in line 1:

```
1  $ pfexec svccfg -s frequent listprop
2  zfs                             application
3  zfs/avoidscrub                  boolean    false
4  zfs/backup-lock                 astring    unlocked
5  zfs/backup-save-cmd             astring    "not set"
6  zfs/fs-name                     astring    //
7  zfs/interval                    astring    minutes
```

continues

```
 8 zfs/label                          astring    frequent
 9 zfs/snapshot-children              boolean    true
10 zfs/verbose                        boolean    true
11 zfs/backup                         astring    none
12 zfs/offset                         astring    0
13 zfs/period                         astring    15
14 zfs/keep                           astring    4
15 general                            framework
16 general/action_authorization       astring    solaris.smf.manage.zfs-auto-snapshot
17 general/value_authorization        astring    solaris.smf.manage.zfs-auto-snapshot
18 general/enabled                    boolean    true
19 restarter                          framework  NONPERSISTENT
20 restarter/logfile                  astring    /var/svc/log/\
system-filesystem-zfs-auto-snapshot:frequent.log
21 restarter/start_pid                count      585
22 restarter/start_method_timestamp   time       1235948503243160000
23 restarter/start_method_waitstatus  integer    0
24 restarter/transient_contract       count
25 restarter/auxiliary_state          astring    none
26 restarter/next_state               astring    none
27 restarter/state                    astring    online
28 restarter/state_timestamp          time       1235948503.264556000
```

The `zfs/period` property on line 13 is currently set to 15, and the `zfs/interval` property on line 7 is set to minutes. The following command line will set the period to ten minutes:

```
$ pfexec svccfg -s frequent setprop zfs/period=10
$ pfexec svccfg -s frequent listprop zfs/period
zfs/period  astring  10
```

Next, reread the instance:

$ **pfexec svccfg -s frequent refresh**

Restart the frequent service:

$ **pfexec svcadm restart frequent**

Check the zfssnap `crontab` to confirm the updated schedule. Now the snapshots occur at a 10-minute interval.

```
1 $ pfexec crontab -l zfssnap
2 0 0 1 1,2,3,4,5,6,7,8,9,10,11,12 * /lib/svc/method/zfs-auto-snapshot\
  svc:/system/filesystem/zfs/auto-snapshot:monthly
3 0 0 1,2,3,4,5,6,7,8,9,10,11,12,13,14,15,\
  16,17,18,19,20,21,22,23,24,25,26,27,28,29,30,31 * *\
  /lib/svc/method/zfs-auto-snapshot svc:/system/filesystem/zfs/\
  auto-snapshot:daily
```

continues

```
4 0 0 1,8,15,22,29 * * /lib/svc/method/zfs-auto-snapshot \
  svc:/system/filesystem/zfs/auto-snapshot:weekly
5 0 0,1,2,3,4,5,6,7,8,9,10,11,12,13,14,15,16,17,18,19,20,21,22,23 * * \
* /lib/svc/method/zfs-auto-snapshot \
  svc:/system/filesystem/zfs/auto-snapshot:hourly
6 0,10,20,30,40,50 * * * * /lib/svc/method/zfs-auto-snapshot \
  svc:/system/filesystem/zfs/auto-snapshot:frequent
```

On line 6, the frequency of the snaps is now changed to every 10 minutes starting at the top of the hour.

7.3.3 Changing the Number of Snapshots Kept

To keep the last hour of changes, the number of snapshots that are kept needs to be increased from four to six. Again, you will use the commands svccfg and svcadm to make the changes and restart the service:

```
$ pfexec svccfg -s frequent setprop zfs/keep=6
$ pfexec svccfg -s frequent listprop zfs/keep
zfs/keep  astring  6
$ pfexec svccfg -s frequent refresh
$ pfexec svcadm restart frequent
```

7.4 Setting the Snapshot Schedule per File System

You can set snapshot schedules independently on each file system. In the following example, the new file system jan has inherited the property autosnapshots turned off. The file system needs only hourly and weekly scheduled snapshots. Use the zfs command to set the autosnapshot properties. The svcadm command restarts the hourly and weekly autosnapshot methods to inherit the changes in the user *jan* file system.

```
$ pfexec zfs create rpool/export/home/jan
$ zfs get com.sun:auto-snapshot rpool/export/home/jan
NAME                   PROPERTY              VALUE SOURCE
rpool/export/home/jan  com.sun:auto-snapshot false inherited from rpool/export/home
$ pfexec zfs com.sun:auto-snapshot:weekly=true  rpool/export/home/jan
$ pfexec zfs com.sun:auto-snapshot:hourly=true  rpool/export/home/jan
$ pfexec svcadm restart hourly weekly
```

8

Creating a ZFS Lab in a Box

The examples in this book were tested on OpenSolaris 2008.11 and Solaris 10 10/08 using Virtual Box 2.1.x and 2.2.0. Virtual Box is a virtualization product that works with the desktop as well as the enterprise. Virtual Box can run multiple virtual machines (VMs) on a single desktop system. In this case, it was used to do installation and testing quickly and easily on a MacBook Pro laptop with 4GB of RAM.

In this chapter, you'll see how to configure a VM to run OpenSolaris with disks to practice ZFS skills. You can use the same host configuration with Solaris 10 10/08. The Virtual Box GUI presented is captured from a MacBook and is slightly different on other host OSs. The VM that will be created has 1GB of RAM and seven virtual disks (two IDE and five SATA) using Virtual Box 2.2. First you will create new disks for the virtual machine, and then you will create the virtual machine and install OpenSolaris. To finish the installation, you will install the Virtual Box Guest Additions package.

This example uses only a small set of the features of Virtual Box. Go to the Virtual Box Web site for more information (www.virtualbox.org). It is free for personal use.

8.1 Creating Virtual Disks with Virtual Media Manager

Virtual Media Manager (VMM) is used to manage hard disks, CD/DVD images, and floppy images. It can create new virtual disks or register disk images with Virtual Box. It will register ISO images or raw floppy images for VMs to use.

In this section, you will see how to create two IDE 16GB disks for boot disks and five SATA 130MB disks for data. For a Solaris installation, a minimum disk size of 16GB is recommended. You can do the installation on a much smaller disk, but this chapter will use 16GB. ZFS requires disks to be a minimum of 128MB. The VMM can create two kinds of virtual disks:

- **Dynamically expanding storage**: A virtual disk that on initialization uses very little physical disk space but will grow dynamically to the size specified as the guest OS uses the disk space
- **Fixed-size storage**: A virtual disk that does not grow and is stored in a file the same size as the virtual hard disk

Use the following steps to select the dynamically expanding disks to save on the physical disk space:

1. Start Virtual Box, and then select File > VMM (see Figure 8.1).

Figure 8.1 Starting Virtual Media Manager from the File menu

2. Once the VMM panel appears, click the New button. Figure 8.2 includes previously created virtual disk images.

3. The Create New Virtual Disk Wizard appears. Click the Next button to get to the Hard Disk Storage Type panel (see Figure 8.3).

   "Dynamically expanding storage" should be selected by default. If it's not, select it before clicking the Next button. The Virtual Disk Location and Size panel is next (see Figure 8.4).

4. Accept the default location of the new virtual disk. The default location depends on the OS type of the host system. Enter **ZFStest.vdi** for the name of the new disk, and make the size 16GB (see Figure 8.4 (2)).

5. Clicking Next, you get the Summary panel (see Figure 8.5).

6. Click Finish to create the new boot disks for the VM. Repeat the sequence, and create another 16GB disk named ZFStest2.vdi.

Now that the boot disks are created, you need to create six 130MB data disks named z0, z1, z2, z3, z4, and z5.

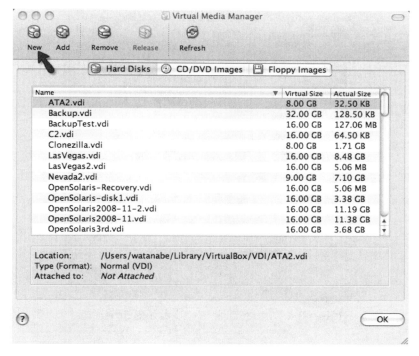

Figure 8.2 VMM panel with the New button highlighted

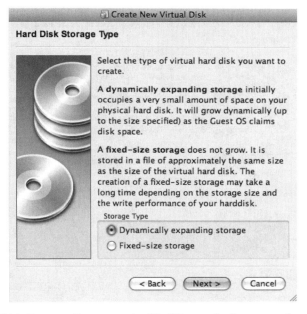

Figure 8.3 Hard Disk Storage Type panel with "Dynamically expanding storage" selected

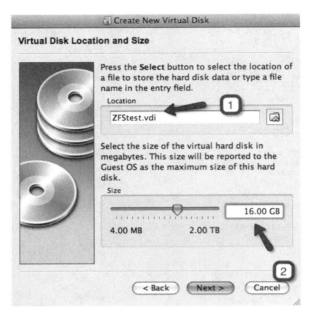

Figure 8.4 Virtual Disk Location and Size panel

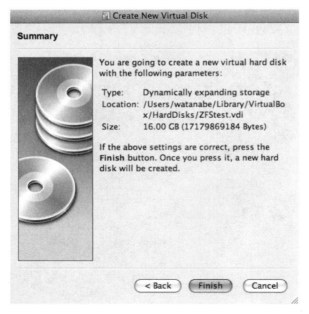

Figure 8.5 Summary panel with the configuration

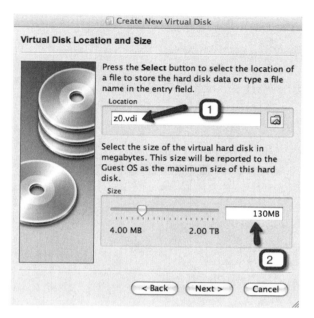

Figure 8.6 Virtual Disk Location and Size panel

1. Name the first disk z0.vdi.
2. Set the size of the disk to 130MB (see Figure 8.6 (2)).
3. After creating the other disks, review them in the VMM panel (see Figure 8.7).

   Figure 8.7 lists all the virtual disks registered to Virtual Box. Notice the actual size of the new data disks of 1.5KB vs. the virtual size.

8.2 Registering a CD Image with Virtual Media Manager

You will need to register the install CD with the VMM. In this case, the CD image is OpenSolaris 2008.11 downloaded from `http://opensolaris.org`. Follow these steps to register it:

1. Click the CD/DVD Images button to get to the registered CD/DVD ISO. Figure 8.8 shows previously registered ISO images.
2. Click the Add button, and locate the installation ISO image. In this example, the OpenSolaris image is `osol-0811.iso`. Figure 8.9 shows the new registered ISO image.

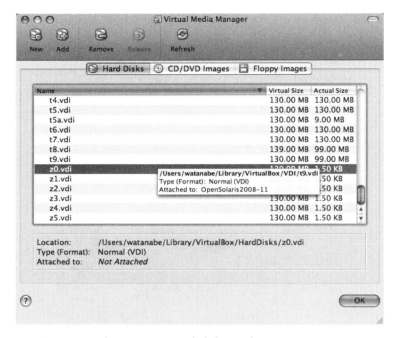

Figure 8.7 Hard disks in the VMM

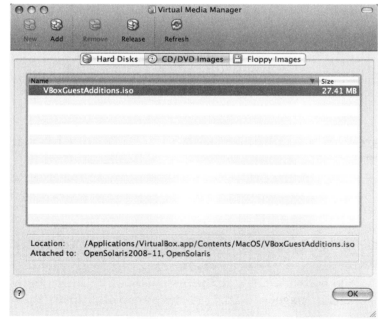

Figure 8.8 Registered ISO images in the VMM

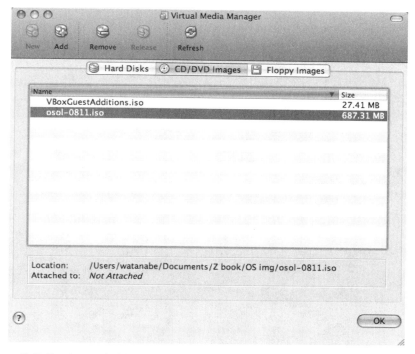

Figure 8.9 Registered ISO images in the VMM with the new OpenSolaris ISO

8.3 Creating a New Virtual Machine

Creating a new VM is the next step in setting up a ZFS lab system. Follow these steps to create the new VM:

1. The main Virtual Box panel (see Figure 8.10) contains a New button at the top left of the panel. The left subpanel is a list of defined systems and status, and the right subpanel has the configuration of each system.

   In the main Virtual Box panel, click the New button to open the Create New Virtual Machine Wizard (see Figure 8.11).

2. Click the Next button to get to the VM Name and OS Type panel (see Figure 8.12).

   For the name of the system, enter **ZFStest** (see Figure 8.12 (1)). For the operating system, select Solaris (see Figure 8.12 (2)). For the version, select OpenSolaris (see Figure 8.12 (3)). Then click the Next button.

3. The next panel configures the memory for the system. Type **1024** in the box for 1GB of physical memory in the VM. Figure 8.13 shows the completed panel.

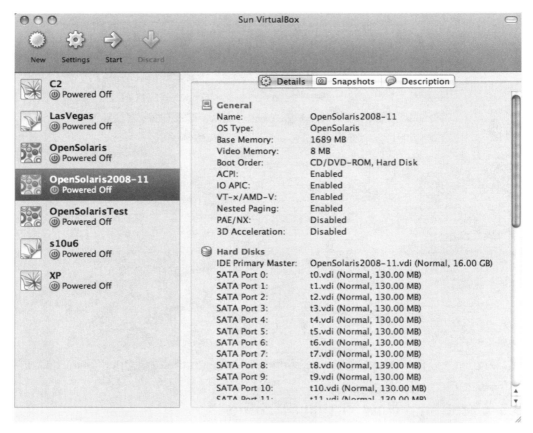

Figure 8.10 Virtual Box main panel

4. Click the Next button to get to the Virtual Hard Disk panel. Because you created the boot disks previously, select "Use existing hard disk." Then select ZFStest.vdi from the menu. Figure 8.14 shows the completed panel.

5. Click the Next button to get to the Summary panel. Check the selection. Then click the Finish button to create the new VM (see Figure 8.15).

   After you click the Finish button, the new VM is created and listed on the left subpanel (see Figure 8.16).

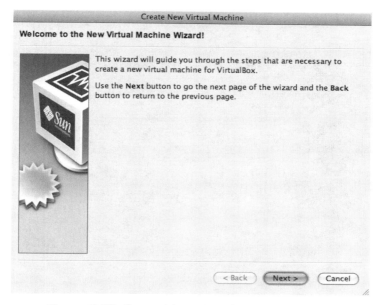

Figure 8.11 Create New Virtual Machine Wizard

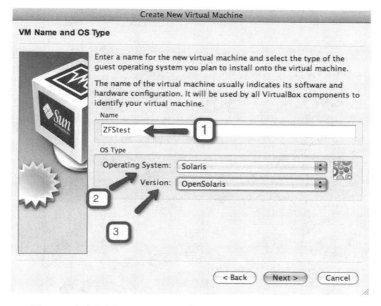

Figure 8.12 VM Name and OS Type panel completed

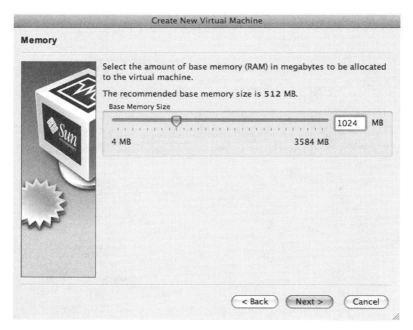

Figure 8.13 The Memory panel with 1024MB

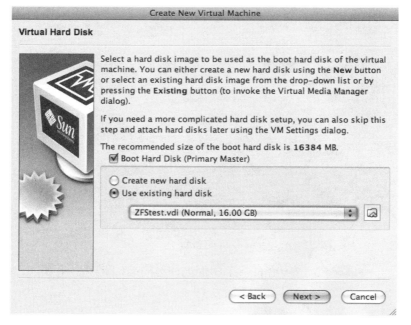

Figure 8.14 Completed Virtual Hard Disk panel with ZFStest.vdi selected

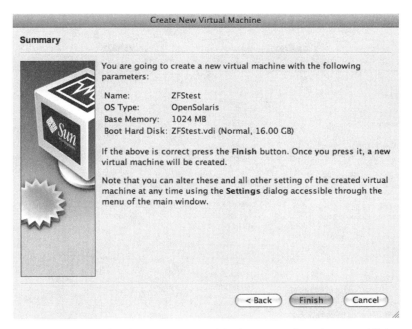

Figure 8.15 The Summary panel before creating the new VM

8.4 Modifying the New Virtual Machine

In this section, you will modify the VM, add new virtual disks, and mount a boot ISO image to the VM:

1. First, select ZFStest on the left panel, and then click the Settings button to open the settings panel for ZFStest. Figure 8.17 shows the General settings for the VM.

2. Click the Storage icon to configure more storage for the VM. Figure 8.18 shows the VM with one disk configured.

3. Add the remaining disks that were previously created to the VM. First, click Enable Additional Controller to add a SATA controller to the VM, and then click the Add Disk icon on the right side of the panel. Match the Slot/Hard Disk pairs for each disk added (see Table 8.1).

   Figure 8.19 shows the completed disk addition and assignments.

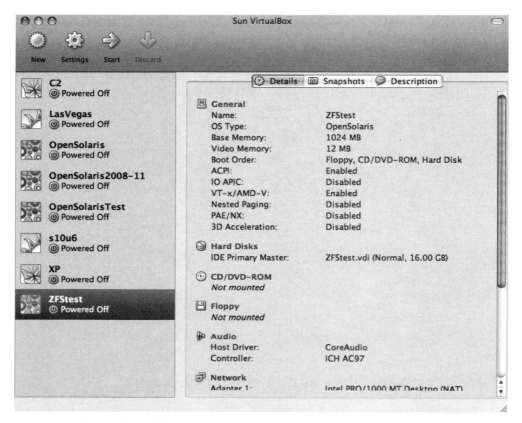

Figure 8.16 The Virtual Box main panel with new ZFStest VM

4. Once the disks have been added to the VM and the SATA assignments have been done, click the OK button. The SATA port assignments can be random, but assigning a numbered disk name to a SATA port number will make it easier to see which disk belongs to which disk target from the OS point of view.

5. Click the CD/DVD-ROM icon. Select Mount CD/DVD Drive. Select ISO Image File. Then select osol-0811.iso from the drop-down menu. Only registered ISO images will be listed. See Figure 8.20 for the completed panel. Click the OK button to complete the configuration.

The ZFStest VM is now completed and ready to boot from the ISO CD image.

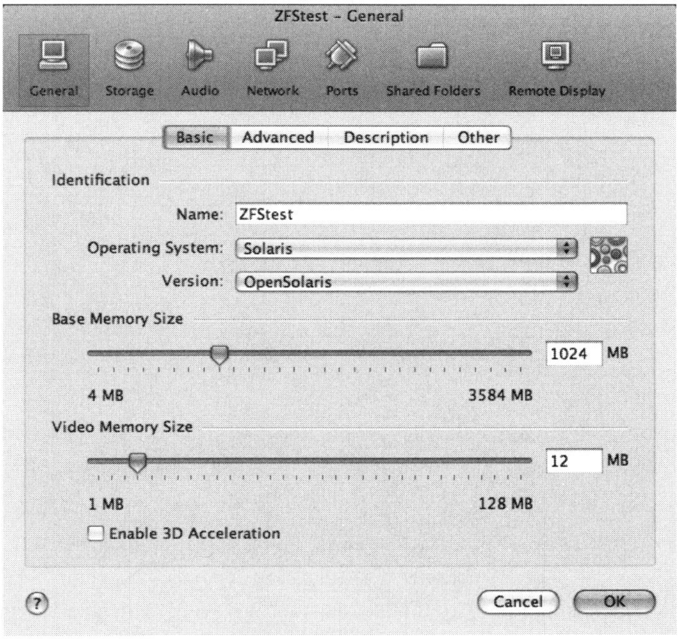

Figure 8.17 The General settings panel for ZFStest VM

Figure 8.18 The Storage settings panel with one disk configured for VM

Table 8.1 Slot and Hard Disk Assignments

Slot	Hard Disk
IDE Secondary	ZFStest2.vdi
SATA Port 0	z0.vdi
SATA Port 1	z1.vdi
SATA Port 2	z2.vdi
SATA Port 3	z3.vdi
SATA Port 4	z4.vdi
SATA Port 5	z5.vdi

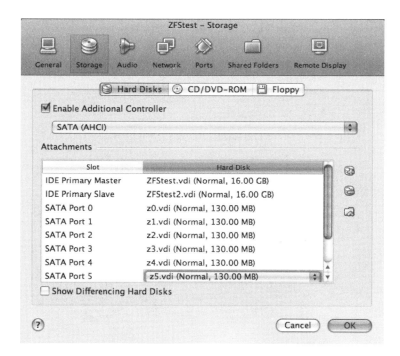

Figure 8.19 New hard disks added to the VM

8.5 Installing an OS on a Virtual Machine

This section covers how to install an operating system on a virtual machine.

To get started, turn on the VM by selecting the Start icon ⤵ at the top of the main panel to start the boot process. Virtual Box will spawn a new window to

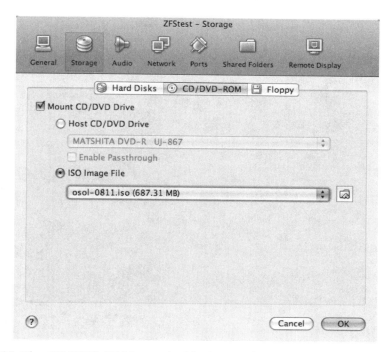

Figure 8.20 The CD/DVD-ROM panel with the ISO boot image mounted on the VM

display the VM running. At this point, the VM will grab the mouse and keyboard. To release both the mouse pointer and keyboard, press the key indicated on the bottom right of the screen. In the MacBook Pro, it is the left Cmd key. On a Solaris host it is the right Ctrl key.

Figure 8.21 shows the icons at the bottom of the Virtual Box VM window. The buttons from left to right are hard disk activity, CD-ROM activity and control, network activity and control, USB control, shared folder, virtualization hardware acceleration status, mouse capture status, and mouse capture key.

Figure 8.21 Icons at the bottom of the VM window

1. A GRUB menu will appear. Select the default GRUB selection. Figure 8.22 shows the GRUB menu from the installation CD.

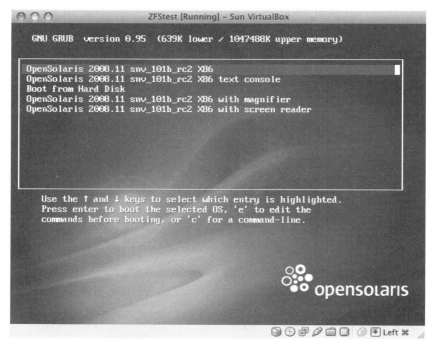

Figure 8.22 The default GRUB menu from the OpenSolaris LiveCD

2. Select your keyboard and language. In this example, just hit the Enter/
   Return key twice. Now the LiveCD will drop into a GNOME session. This is a
   working OpenSolaris system.

3. Double-click Install OpenSolaris to start the install process, as shown in
   Figure 8.23.

4. The first screen is the Welcome screen shown in Figure 8.24. Click the Next
   button to continue.

5. The installer asks a few questions before the actual install. The first question
   is about the disk. By default the first 16GB disk will be selected. Select "Use
   the whole disk." The completed screen should look like Figure 8.25.

6. Click the Next button to get the Time Zone screen. Select your local time zone
   either by using the drop-down menus or by locating a city in your time zone,
   in this case Denver, Colorado (see Figure 8.26).

Figure 8.23 VM ZFStest in LiveCD mode

7. Click the Next button to move on to the Locale screen. In Figure 8.27, English is the default language.

8. Click the Next button to get to the Users screen. Select a password for the root user. Create a username for yourself, and set the password. At this point, you can change the name of the system or leave it as opensolaris. Figure 8.28 shows the completed Users screen.

9. Click the Next button to move to the Installation review screen. This is the last chance to review the installation parameters before the installation procedure begins. See Figure 8.29 for an example.

    The installation will take a few minutes to complete, depending on the host system. You can watch the splash screen for information on the features of OpenSolaris. The completion bar at the bottom will indicate what percent of the installation has completed (see Figure 8.30).

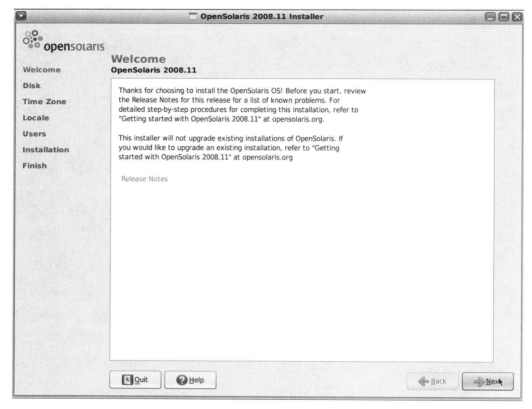

Figure 8.24 Installer at the Welcome screen

10. Once the install is complete, the Finished screen appears, as shown in Figure 8.31. Click the Reboot button to restart the VM with the newly installed OpenSolaris OS.

11. After clicking the Reboot button, the system will reboot from the CD-ROM ISO image. The GRUB menu will appear. Use the down arrow key to scroll down to the Boot from Hard Disk item, and press the Return/Enter key to start the OS from the hard disk. In Figure 8.32 the Boot from Hard Disk item is selected.

12. When you press Enter/Return to boot the OS, another GRUB screen appears. This GRUB menu comes from the hard disk installation. Let the default GRUB selection boot by pressing Enter/Return, or let the timer run down to boot the OS.

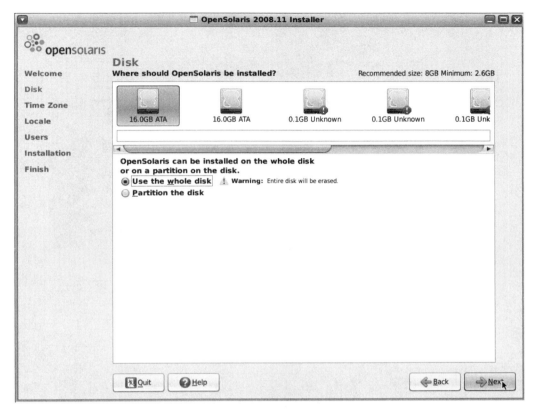

Figure 8.25 The installer at the Disk screen with "Use the whole disk" selected

8.6 Installing Virtual Box Tools

Installing the Virtual Box tools will complete the installation of the OS. There is a different VB tool installation for each of the various OSs that VB supports. The VB tools will enable the VM to seamlessly share the mouse and keyboard and install a video device driver. The video device driver will enable you to resize the VM screen on your host system much like any other application.

1. You need to mount the Virtual Box Guest Additions CD image. First, log in to OpenSolaris as the user defined during the installation. Next, right-click (on a Mac, Cmd+click) the OpenSolaris CD icon on the desktop. Select Unmount Volume to unmount the CD image. In Figure 8.33, Unmount Volume is selected from the drop-down menu.

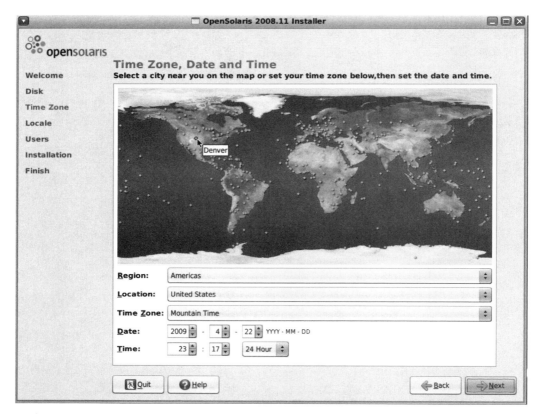

Figure 8.26 The installer at the Time Zone screen with Denver, Colorado, selected

2. You need to mount the Virtual Box Guest Additions CD image. Once the CD image is unmounted, free your mouse from the VM using the mouse capture key indicated at the bottom-right corner of the window. Now move the mouse pointer over the CD-ROM icon at the bottom of the screen, and click the icon. Select CD/DVD-ROM Image, as shown in Figure 8.34.

3. The Virtual Media Manager window is now displayed. Select the VirtualBoxAdditions.iso image, and click the Select button. In Figure 8.35, the VMM window is open with the Virtual Box Guest Additions image selected.

   If the image does not mount, go to the CD-ROM icon at the bottom of the VM window, select the physical CD-ROM, and then repeat the selection of the image file.

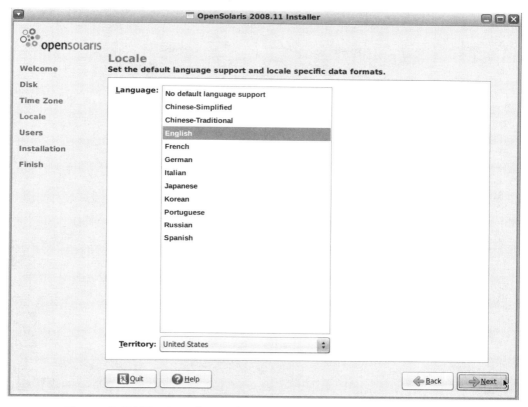

Figure 8.27 The installer at the Locale screen with English selected

4. When the image is mounted, a warning message box is displayed. Click the Run button to continue with the mount.

5. The Virtual Box Guest Additions CD image must be installed from the command line. Open a terminal window by clicking the Terminal icon on the top menu bar.

6. Change directories to /media/VBOXADDITIONS_2.2.0_45846. The *VBOX* directory may be different depending on the build you download from http://virtualbox.org.
    ```
    $ cd /media/VBOX*
    ```

7. Install the guest package VBoxSolarisAdditions.pkg using the following command line. Because this install needs root privileges, the command needs to start with the command pfexec. The user defined in the install

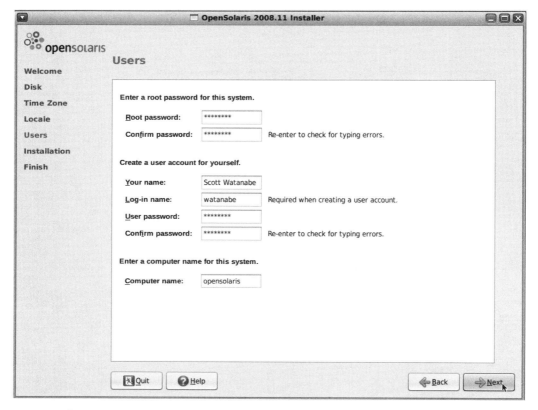

Figure 8.28 The installer at the Users screen with the fields completed

will have root privileges defined by the Solaris Role-Based Access Control (RBAC) facility. See the man page on RBAC, or go to `http://docs.sun.com` for more information on RBAC.

```
$ pfexec pkgadd -d VBoxSolarisAdditions.pkg
```

8. Press Enter/Return, and answer *y* for yes to install the package. Log out of the system by clicking System on the top menu bar and selecting Log Out. See Figure 8.36 for the menu.

9. Log in again to activate the VB Guest Additions image. Now your OpenSolaris system is ready to be your ZFS lab in a box.

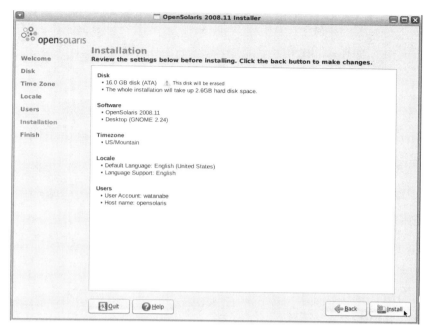

Figure 8.29 The installer at the Installation review screen

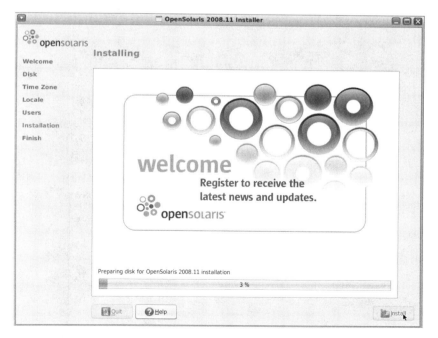

Figure 8.30 The installer loading OpenSolaris

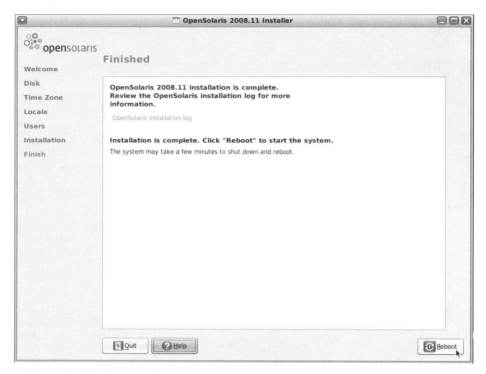

Figure 8.31 The installer Finished screen after the installation is completed

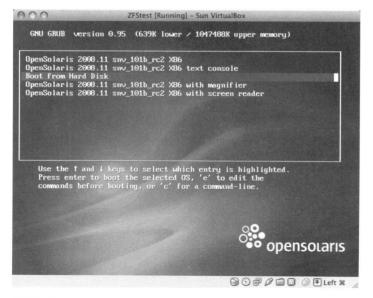

Figure 8.32 The GRUB menu with the Boot from Hard Disk item selected

Figure 8.33 The mouse right-click menu with Unmount Volume selected

Figure 8.34 CD icon drop-down menu with CD/DVD-ROM Image selected

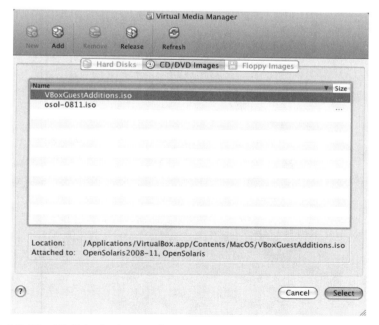

Figure 8.35 The VMM window with Virtual Box Guest Additions image selected
to be mounted

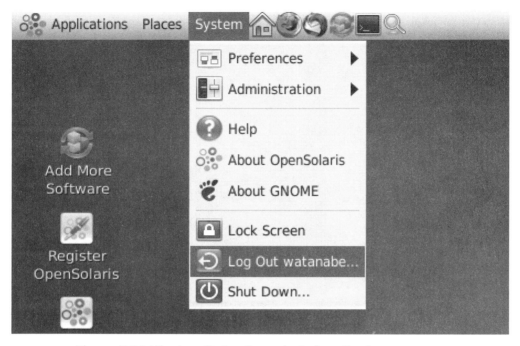

Figure 8.36 The Log Out action selected on the System menu

Index

Solaris™ 10 System Administration Essentials

ISBN-13: 978-0-13-700009-8

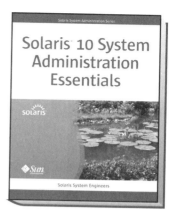

Solaris™ 10 System Administration Essentials is the first book to concisely yet comprehensively cover all of the breakthrough features of the Solaris 10 operating system. The Solaris OS has a long history of innovation, and the Solaris 10 OS is a watershed release that includes features such as Zones, ZFS™, the Fault Management Architecture, the Service Management Facility, and Dynamic Tracing (DTrace). In addition, the Solaris 10 OS fully supports 32-bit and 64-bit x86 platforms, as well as the SPARC® architecture.

The book's key topics include

- Installing, booting, and shutting down a system
- Managing packages and patches (software updates)
- Controlling system processes
- Managing disks and devices
- Managing users
- Configuring networks
- Using printing services

Solaris™ 10 System Administration Essentials is a practical guide to deploying and managing the Solaris 10 operating system in a business or academic environment. The book is easy to read and rich with examples—a perfect companion for system administrators who are deploying the Solaris OS for the first time.

informit.com/title/9780137000098

Solaris™ 10 Security Essentials

ISBN-13: 978-0-13-701233-6

Solaris™ 10 Security Essentials describes the various security technologies contained in the Solaris operating system. The book describes how to make installations secure and how to configure the OS to the particular needs of your environment, whether your systems are on the edge of the Internet or running a data center. The authors present the material in a straightforward way that makes a seemingly arcane subject accessible to system administrators at all levels.

The strengths of the Solaris operating system's security model are its scalability and its adaptability. It can protect a single user with login authentication or multiple users with Internet and intranet configurations requiring user-rights management, authentication, encryption, IP security, key management, and more. This book is written for users who need to secure their laptops, network administrators who must secure an entire company, and everyone in between.

The book's topics include

- Zones virtualization security
- System hardening
- Trusted Extensions (Multilevel Security)
- Privileges and role-based access control (RBAC)
- Cryptographic services and key management
- Auditing
- Network security
- Pluggable Authentication Modules (PAM)

Solaris™ 10 Security Essentials is a superb guide to deploying and managing secure computer environments.

informit.com/title/9780137012336

PRENTICE HALL

informit.com/ph

inform T.com THE TRUSTED TECHNOLOGY LEARNING SOURCE

PEARSON **InformIT** is a brand of Pearson and the online presence for the world's leading technology publishers. It's your source for reliable and qualified content and knowledge, providing access to the top brands, authors, and contributors from the tech community.

Addison-Wesley   Cisco Press   EXAM/**CRAM**   **IBM** Press.   QUe·   :: PRENTICE HALL   S**A**MS | Safari"

LearnIT at InformIT

Looking for a book, eBook, or training video on a new technology? Seeking timely and relevant information and tutorials? Looking for expert opinions, advice, and tips? **InformIT has the solution.**

- Learn about new releases and special promotions by subscribing to a wide variety of newsletters. Visit **informit.com/newsletters**.

- Access FREE podcasts from experts at **informit.com/podcasts**.

- Read the latest author articles and sample chapters at **informit.com/articles**.

- Access thousands of books and videos in the Safari Books Online digital library at **safari.informit.com**.

- Get tips from expert blogs at **informit.com/blogs**.

Visit **informit.com/learn** to discover all the ways you can access the hottest technology content.

Are You Part of the **IT** Crowd?

Connect with Pearson authors and editors via RSS feeds, Facebook, Twitter, YouTube, and more! Visit **informit.com/socialconnect**.

inform T.com THE TRUSTED TECHNOLOGY LEARNING SOURCE   **PEARSON**

Addison-Wesley   **Cisco Press**   EXAM/**CRAM**   **IBM** Press.   QUe·   :: PRENTICE HALL   S**A**MS | Safari"